'The Sahel is one of the most  t
contains many of the most inte r
Hudson's lyrical book about th l
helping for the last 20 years gi s
these brave people face and ge. ...., ... ve
helped to overcome them.'

Robin Hanbury-Tenison, explorer and founder of Survival International

'This is written by a man who knows the parts of Africa he writes of better than almost any other Western author. Peter Hudson addresses his experiences in Africa with a searing honesty and refreshing insight. He is not blind to the continent's difficulties and shortcomings. Nor does he fall prey to the simplistic romanticism of so many travellers. But he clearly loves Africa and his affection shines through his writing. Before packing their bags for Africa, development workers, charity workers, diplomats, journalists and travellers should read Hudson's account of his undertaking in West Africa and then ponder their own motives and mission.'

Alec Russell, an editor at the *Financial Times* and author of *After Mandela.*

'I loved this book and it stayed with me for a long time. His present-tense account of a visit to Mauritania to monitor the progress of his small-scale aid projects is vivid, humble, deeply felt and at times incredibly moving. He writes with a freshness and a lack of artifice that is beyond the pretence of most travel writing – as if he, and we, were seeing the world entirely afresh. The result is quietly wonderful.'

Roger Crowley, author of *Constantinople* and *Empires of the Sea.*

'Impoverished agricultural communities in Mauritania, and especially in marginal areas prone to desertification after the great droughts of the 1970s and 1980s, need to rely on "stable governments, stable market prices and a stable climate, none of which are currently very available". At the heart of Peter Hudson's book is a rallying cry for the restoration of trust and confidence in the people and land of Mauritania, together with a practical demonstration of how that can be achieved by the patience, sensitivity, idealism and determination of Mauritanians themselves working to overcome a despair that nothing will ever change. In the course of the book, the hot sweet metallic taste of the mint tea – over which a fascinating swirl of characters is conjured to give us insights into social life, cultural and religious outlooks and the conflicted history of Mauritania – becomes a taste for the people themselves, how much their pride and resilience, humility and hospitality are admired and trusted.'

Gabriel Gbadamosi, Nigerian poet, playwright and novelist, author of *Vauxhall*.

'An Englishman sets up a series of grassroots projects in Mauritania with a local friend… the question is: can things ever change? Hudson's account of rural life in Mauritania delivers a great cast of characters, the color and texture of their lives vibrantly described… the rituals of daily life of desert people lovingly and entertainingly conveyed. Off the beaten track doesn't begin to cover it: this is an unexpected, intimate view of village life, of people ravaged by war and drought, determined to survive.'

Clare Longrigg, author and *Guardian* editor.

UNDER AN AFRICAN SKY

A journey to the frontline of climate change

About the author

Peter Hudson has worked as a farmer, charity worker, travel writer and photographer. Over a period of 30 years, he has travelled extensively throughout Africa, visiting 31 countries, the majority of them seen from the back of a bush-taxi, donkey or moped. He has written three previous books about Africa. The first of these – *A Leaf in the Wind* (Columbus Books, 1988), which details a year-long journey made from Morocco to Egypt via West, Central and East Africa – was nominated for the 1989 Thomas Cook Travel Book of the Year award. His second book, *Travels in Mauritania*, was published in 1990 by Virgin Books. His third book, *Two Rivers*, recounts the story of following in the footsteps of British explorer Mungo Park, the first European to discover the Niger River in what is today Mali. Peter currently lives with his family on the Herefordshire/Wales border.

UNDER AN AFRICAN SKY

A journey to the frontline of climate change

PETER HUDSON

New Internationalist

Under An African Sky
First published in 2014 by
New Internationalist Publications Ltd
The Old Music Hall
106-108 Cowley Road
Oxford OX4 1JE, UK
newint.org

Front cover photos: Peter Hudson; Tony P Eveling/Alamy

Printed by TJ International Ltd, Cornwall, UK
who hold environmental accreditation ISO 14001.

British Library Cataloguing-in-Publication Data
A catalogue record for this book is available from the British Library.

Library of Congress Cataloging-in-Publication Data
A catalog record for this book is available from the Library of Congress.

ISBN 978-1-78026-178-2

Dedication

For Marie, Ruby, Caitlin, Rosabel and Eile.

Acknowledgements
I would like to thank the people of the Islamic Republic of Mauritania for their unfailingly good-humored hospitality. I would like to thank all those many people who, over the years, I have seen and met on roadsides, in villages and on city streets from whom I have learned so much. In the UK, I would like to thank both Michael Marten and Laura Longrigg for reading my manuscript and giving me encouragement; Chris Brazier, my editor at New Internationalist for correcting my many mistakes (and bringing me up to date on certain matters of expression!); Veronica, my sister, for her brilliant drawings; and my wife, Marie, for her constant support (and her proofreading skills!). For reasons of anonymity and security the names of people and of some places mentioned in this book have been altered.

Donation
A portion of the royalties from the sales of this book will be used for our ongoing development work in southern Mauritania.

Contents

The Islamic Republic of Mauritania

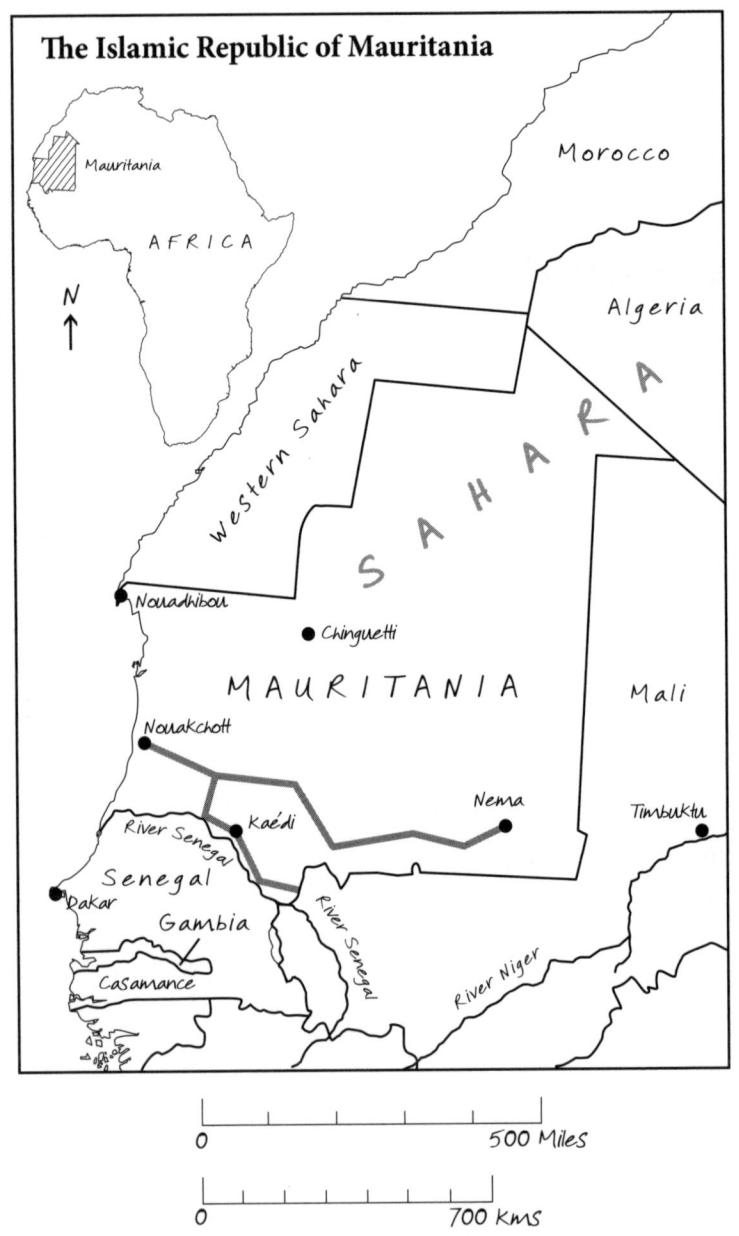

Introduction

A bush taxi in the south of Mauritania, West Africa. Outside, wastes of sand and scrub; a fierce wind. This is the Sahel, the southern 'shore' of the Sahara: a region at the frontline of climate change. I am sandwiched in the back of the vehicle's three rows of seats between two large men. Up front sits a man of about my age: 28. He is clean-shaven, with a look of calm and gentleness about him. Beside him sits a girl of five or six, his daughter, perhaps: a picture of the prettiest and most composed perfection. With her hair plaited immaculately to her scalp, her African print dress wrapped neatly to the ankles and her hands folded demurely in her lap, she looks more like a mini-adult than a child. The man, I notice, treats her as such.

It is 1988 and I am travelling aimlessly: a well-stocked backpack, money in my pocket and time on my hands. I have taken the taxi south only because it is one of the few parts of Mauritania I have not yet seen. By camel, donkey, foot and bush-taxi, I have travelled the length and breadth of this desert country. I have been to the ancient caravan towns stuck far out in the desert with their ancient libraries and smells of the Maghreb. I have stayed with nomads, sharing their ghee and couscous, drinking milk last thing at night, warm from the udders of their cows. I have seen and experienced a great many aspects of this wild, dusty and difficult country, not least the 'White' Moors – those supreme desert opportunists now trying their hands at modernity and all the angles of gain and exploitation it can provide the quick-witted – and the 'Black' Moors, descendants of freed slaves, at best sharing the power and spoils of nationhood with their white-hued, clannish compatriots; at worst, subsisting at the bottom of the pile with a handful of goats and a scrap of tent.

In the towns and cities, the roux of black, white and brown, of traders, marketeers and shanty-dwellers, was infinite and infinitely fascinating. Here was a world turned inside-out: all the mechanisms of an economy and society – the industry, ingenuity, joy and suffering – displayed in all their raw vitality: a man hammering satellite dishes out of pieces of sheet metal; an entire street of blackened charcoal sellers; an alleyway of settees; water sellers; ragged madmen; letter writers by the post office; infants defecating on curbs; an anarchy of fuming vehicles swarming like an invasion of locusts down and into every passage, road and alleyway. And among them, I, a lone Westerner – for I only rarely saw another Westerner – wandered freely, never once threatened or alienated. Then I decided to travel south.

This was where the Black Africans lived, in country where more precipitation meant a degree of agriculture and so a different existence. These were the Bantu peoples of sub-Saharan Africa – as opposed to the desert-dwelling Moors, whose culture harks back to the Berbers of North Africa and the Yemeni Arabs who invaded Mauritania in the 17th century. These two peoples – the intensely clannish Moorish dwellers of the desert and the Bantu to their south – have been traditional rivals ever since, and the frontline of their rivalry

has always been the band of country along the southern edge of the Sahara: the Sahel. This is where desert finally gives way to scrub. It is where pastures, born of the annual rains, can take a better hold, where rain-fed agriculture is possible, and where seasonal rivers and streams can sometimes be found.

I had barely spoken to that young man during the journey south; perhaps just some pleasantries exchanged during one of the innumerable stops. Then, amid the swirling confusion of dusk and dust in Kaédi, the regional capital, where the bush taxi deposited us, the young man asked if I would like to accompany him to his village. I must have looked a little lost, standing beside my backpack in the taxi park.

'Yes,' I said, 'I'd like to very much.'

'My name is Salif,' he said, 'and this,' he indicated his pretty young daughter standing by his side, 'is Ramata.'

And, because Salif was an honest man – as even then I could see – I believed him when he told me his village was not far. Two hours later, after a nightmarish journey lurching along a concrete-hard track, squeezed into the back of a taxi-van with 30 other souls, we arrived. But I am glad I accepted Salif's offer. For it was here that I first became acquainted with Mustapha, Abu and Harouna... with Fama, Mariam and Aliou... with Amuna and Isa and Musa... all those many people whose lives in the 25 subsequent years – in most of which I have paid them a visit – have unfolded in step with my own. Some, at that time, were mere babes in arms. Some, who were youngsters, are now at the forefront of family affairs. Some have long gone grey and settled back into the quiet anonymity of elderhood; and some have died – too many. On that first trip, though, Mamadou, Amadou and Mohamedou were names I could not untangle, especially when their owners were little more than profiles in the darkness of the village night, only a sheen of expression visible in the starlight.

Images have stayed with me from that first trip to Salif's village: a naked child squatting by an open ditch of effluent, chewing on a dried chicken bone he had just picked up; a boy perched on a donkey-cart, setting about his poor, emaciated beast with a stick like a truncheon, beating its bruised and sore-covered back until its knees buckled and it crumpled up; Salif's mother, with a strong arm and a gleam in her eye, milking a cow whose ribs stuck out like a plate rack. But then this was poor country. It had been devastated by the great Sahelian droughts of the 1970s and 1980s, during which 90 per cent of the livestock of its pastoralist inhabitants had perished. Losing 90 per cent of herds that represented all a family's wealth and inheritance and have been built up over generations was devastating. At one fell swoop, these once proud livestock herders were robbed of the means and, indeed, the very purpose of existence. The herds they now had were pitiful reminders of what they had once possessed, and they relied instead on a rain-fed agriculture that even in good years could never pay the bills.

Yet Salif's family, despite the obvious difficulty of their condition, were the 'wealthy' ones. They and their like, I was to discover, were the ones to whom other families – those in the camps and hamlets in the bush – looked up. It was they who inhabited the large home-village where the markets, the schools, the medical center and the administrative representatives were to be found. It was to these bigger, patron

families that poorer cousins from the bush would send any promising children so they could study the Qu'ran or go to the primary school. It was to these families they would come when they were desperate: for support, assistance, food. Poverty, I realized – besides being highly subjective – was also relative.

I was struck by the hardship of the region in a way I never had been before, but I was also charmed by a culture that was gentler, subtler and more disciplined than the many cultures I had already been charmed by in the continent. Perhaps it was that special blend of Bantu Africa with Islam which is so clearly delineated in the Sahel, the first perhaps softening the sharper edges of the second, the second perhaps calming the more fiery temperament of the first. Perhaps it was the merging of the pastoral, semi-nomadic peoples of the plains with the more settled agrarian culture of those to the south. Perhaps it was the history of the cultured civilizations that had been born of the wealthy trans-Sahara trade at whose terminus the Sahel was situated – empires such as ancient Ghana, great Mali and Songhai. These had standing armies hundreds of thousands strong, universities to which students travelled from as far away as North Africa, and centralized bureaucracies: an inheritance that can be seen in the the

Sahelian peoples' bearing of inner confidence and calm. Or perhaps it was just the wide-open, fenceless country, softened at the edges by sand, with horizons, like those at sea, promising anonymity and a clear space in which to breathe.

Whichever, of all of the parts of Africa I have visited, it is to this dusty and, in many respects, unspectacular corner that, time and again, I have been drawn back. Salif and I now run small development projects there. And each year, grey winter approaching, I board a plane to emerge, four hours later, under a bright African sky.

1 The Capital

Morning in Nouakchott... Why I come back year after year... Salif's brave return home... Monsieur Adrosso and the de-husker dilemma... A visit to the Cinquième market

4.30am: I am jolted awake by a muezzin calling the early prayers – an overly amplified, ugly sound coming from the mosque just down the street. The sound wavers on, sometimes descending into a chant, at others, reasserting itself. I drift in and out of sleep.

5.45am: Amadou's radio bursts to life. Amadou is the owner of the house in which I am staying, out by the sand dunes on the edge of town. He is hard of hearing, so the French news program he listens to always each morning is played at full volume. I listen as he goes about preparing himself for work: the clink of tea glasses, a noisy hacking in the yard, mumbled conversations with his wife. In my room, it is pitch dark.

6.30am: The metal yard door scrapes open as Amadou leaves for work and a moment later his vehicle, parked directly outside the door, is gunned explosively to life. Shortly, the students wake up. I hear them move about: clumping, hacking, drawing water from the water jar just outside my door. There are always any number of students and other miscellaneous

family members staying at 'L'Auberge Amadou', as I call it. The students do not take breakfast and I soon hear the yard door scraping open again as they make off to the main thoroughfare into town beside which they will wait with all the other early morning wraiths for a taxi-van to pick them up. A thin light is just starting to illuminate my room.

Amadou's wife, Fama, begins cleaning pots and pans in the yard, clanking and banging them against each other. In my mind's eye I can see her, squatting on a small stool in the yard, dress stretched tightly between her knees, bent over the huge pots as she scrubs them inside and out. Fama is young with dark eyes and a shy manner. Beside her, Isata, her daughter, sits on the ground teething on a nice, sharp bottle top. For a while Fama sings a quiet song until interrupted by a man calling in the compound doorway. A loud, shouty conversation ensues, interspersed with periodic bursts of laughter, the babble of rounded, tumbling syllables going on and on. This is the Peul language, of which I understand little.

8.00am: A herd of sheep stops outside my window, bleating loudly.

8.15am: Ghettoblaster music erupts from a neighbor. God, I've forgotten how noisy Africa is.

I wake finally mid-morning but I do not immediately get

up, as it is my first day this year back in Nouakchott, capital of Mauritania, and I did not make it to bed until 4am. It is true, one part of me is itching to get going, as there is much to do on my first day back, and I am eager to get out and see the African day. Another part of me, though, is in a soft, holiday mode. The light in my shuttered room now, thin as it still is, has an orange hue that speaks of a tropical sun. Coming from grey, northern climes, I am conditioned to relax in such light.

I lie on my foam mattress and think about how it all started.

You could say it started in 1991, the year I received my first letter from Salif. His family were in a bad way at that time, a third successive year of poor-to-non-existent rains having left them virtually destitute, with nothing to fall back on. They had little left even to eat, and the wages Salif earned at the mining company where he worked in the north of the country could not feed the great many mouths there were back in the village. Not that Salif, typically, mentioned any of this in his letter. All he said then was that he wondered if I might help his family find the finances for an irrigation project, as they did not have the means to finance it themselves. I was very welcome, he said, to come and see them again, when he could further explain his plans to me. I was looking for an excuse to get back to Africa and so agreed to make the journey.

It turned out to be a bad moment for the people of southern Mauritania, for it had only been in 1989, two years previously, that the military dictatorship that then ruled the country had used a border dispute with its southerly neighbor, Senegal, as an excuse to impose a period of ethnic cleansing against its southern minority Black African population – expelling them from all positions of responsibility, imprisoning a great many, killing many hundreds, if not thousands, and ejecting another 100,000 from the country.

I arrived only some months after the end of this period but again, typically of Salif, and typically also of myself, I travelled all the way to the village in the south – into what was virtually a war zone at the time, with tensions on both sides very high and the army mounting roadblocks every few kilometers – completely ignorant of what had taken place. This was both because I was not at that time in the habit of finding out about places before I went to them, and because Salif's natural diffidence prohibited him from mentioning it. Indeed, it was not until many years later that I realized just how closely my trip had coincided with this traumatic period of oppression.

And so it began. I helped Salif's family purchase a water pump. Some time later, a second pump was added; then a tractor. And then, in the year 2000, Salif announced that he wished to give up his job in the north and return to his village to concentrate on agriculture. He wanted, he said, not only to develop his family's irrigation project but also to see what he could do to help agriculture in the region as a whole.

This was a move that made me nervous for Salif. He would be giving up a secure job and an income, both rarities in the country. And for what: the uncertainties of agriculture in one of the most marginalized, climatically challenged and poorest parts of the world. But he was adamant. He had no doubt. He did not want to pass away his life in an office on some meaningless clerical job where, because of his ethnicity, there was no hope of promotion.

'In the south I can be a farmer,' he said. 'Here, I am nothing.'

So it was that Salif returned to his village, which was an action of both courage and rarity in Africa, where those who have managed to get an education and a job do not often return to their homes. We agreed that if he looked for worthwhile agricultural projects, I would see if I could find funds to support them. And over the years this is more or less what has happened. Salif now runs a small development group based in his home village, or small town, of Keniéba; I help him create the projects and look for the funds for them.

It is Salif, of course, who has borne the brunt of this work. It is he who has had to juggle the many, often irreconcilable, requirements involved in our actions. It is easy to underestimate how difficult things can be in countries such as Mauritania. Small but often essential actions that we in the developed world take for granted – like walking into a garage and buying a new car tire, for example, or withdrawing some money from a bank, or popping over to discuss a matter with a neighbor – in developing countries can take on gargantuan proportions of effort that seemingly quite outweigh the gain. One time it took Salif six months to locate a replacement tire for our four-wheel drive, which cost him $450. A bank might, if you're lucky, let you open an account and put money into it, but when you come to withdraw it again you could well find yourself facing an extortionate 'fee' to do so. And the trip to see the neighbor – even if you are lucky enough to have access to a vehicle – might well involve having to first source some fuel, then negotiate a police post, and next an area swamped with flood waters, while all the time carrying in the back three family members with commissions of their own, meaning countless diversions, not to mention picking up on the way two men with six sheep who are relations of the driver's and need delivering somewhere else. Then you might get a puncture, and have no spare. And that's just the journey there.

So, planning and implementing projects that require participatory consultations, risk and impact assessments, log frames and baseline data, not to mention all the infrastructure development and financial or people management requirements. But Salif, despite his quiet, unassuming manner, is a resourceful man and somehow –

often I have no idea how – things just seem to work out. This has taken a lot of work, though, and for Salif by far the most intense and trying parts of this endeavor coincide with my annual visits.

By the time I open my bedroom door onto Amadou's small yard, the sun is already high. I perform my ablutions in the toilet cubicle by the yard door; then brush my teeth under the yard tree. Salif and his brother, Amadou Tall, who is our driver, are dozing on divans in the lounge, their *bobos* pulled over their heads against the flies. Salif sits up as I enter. He asks how I slept.

'Not so good,' I reply, speaking French, the language in which I communicate in Mauritania. 'The muezzin was up very early this morning.'

'Too early,' Salif agrees. Then his face darkens. 'These Islamists,' he spits out. 'They are not good Muslims. All they want to do is impress people with their devoutness. But the Qu'ran says only that we must pray before dawn, not in the middle of the night.'

There are not many things that outwardly stir Salif, but this, I have discovered, is one of them. He does not like Islam, his religion, to be misrepresented.

We take breakfast on the floor in the lounge – coffee and baguette – and discuss all that has to be accomplished during the 11 days of my visit. It is a long list: it is a year since I was here. We have a large seminar organized in Salif's village to which a Senegalese consultant will be coming, poled over the Senegal River in a dugout. This is a new direction for us: never before have we brought in outside help and we do not know how it will work out. We too will have to cross into Senegal by dugout – avoiding border posts, if we can – to see our Dohley Women's Market Garden project, with which there are issues related to 'mission drift'. There are also problems with our well-digging program and the provision – or rather lack – of donkeys for hauling. Then there are questions over the sustainability of certain tractor services we provide, school desks that have not materialized... there is much to fit in over the next few days.

As always in the capital, Salif is dressed in a smart white bobo, as the traditional Mauritanian gown is known: as brilliant and immaculate as some rare and elegant seabird. He hoists the excess folds of material over his shoulder and dips his baguette into his tea. We are discussing Ibrahim Tandia, the Senegalese development consultant who will be leading our seminar.

'He's coming over the river,' Salif says.

'He's arriving soon?' I ask.

'In four days' time,' Salif says.

'Coming to Kaédi?'

'Yes,' Salif replies. 'The Dohley women will bring him over the river.'

'So he will go to their village?' I ask.

'Yes, he'll go there first, arriving in the afternoon, and they'll bring him over.'

'At the official border crossing?'

Salif nods his head, chewing his bread: 'Yes, at the border crossing.'

'So he can get an official stamp in his passport?'

'Of course.'

'And we'll meet him in town?'

Salif smiles. 'Of course.' Not a flicker of impatience has crossed his face.

In all the years I have known Salif, he has changed little. He has put on a little weight; and at times his face has the puffy, strained look of the overworked, for, as well as having responsibility for all our development efforts and any number of income-generating and agricultural activities, Salif is also head of a large extended family, and as such faces multitudinous extra pressures and duties. But that same air of calm and gentleness that drew me to him when I first met him all those years ago has not changed at all.

It is nearing midday by the time we leave Amadou's and the sun is bright as I step out the yard door. Its rays are warm on my skin and I feel the layers of winter peeling away. Outside stands our vehicle: a double-cab four-wheel drive Toyota pick-up. It is battered beyond belief – strapped up and shattered – and I am reminded of the importance of replacing it. Our work would be impossible without a vehicle. In the early days, we made do with public transport and donkey-carts. This was tiring and limiting, however, and turning up at a village or an irrigation scheme in a donkey-cart did not do a lot for Salif's credibility.

Amadou Tall is standing near the Toyota tinkering with one of the non-functioning windows. He is an ex-truck driver: a tougher, more roughened version of his elder brother. I ask him whether he thinks the Toyota will last much longer.

'Of course,' he replies, a little brusquely. I cannot tell if he actually believes this. I have doubts as to whether it will even survive the duration of my visit. As if to confirm this, when we climb in to depart, the vehicle will not start. The

engine cover is lifted, under which Amadou Tall disappears for a while amidst much banging. We get out and push, and it coughs into life.

'The injection pump,' Amadou Tall remarks nonchalantly as we climb back in.

The capital opens up as we make our way into it: a city at first glance of sand and rubbish and people who do not know how to drive. It is as if the desert simply continues here in the town. Vehicles use any part of it that is not actually built on: sidewalks, passageways, markets, people's yards. The larger roads consist of floods of vehicles, which, at intersections, grind violently into each other. So entirely anarchic and un-municipally minded are the ex-desert dwellers behind the wheels of these vehicles, so wholly unable are they to conform to even the most commonsensical rules of the road, that it is not uncommon at a junction to end up in a traffic jam consisting of only three vehicles, all so completely insistent on not giving way that they draw closer and closer to each other until they create a mini gridlock all of their own. At such moments, a little despair comes over me. I look around and I can see only venality: the large, bearded desert man in his tall four-by-four, contempt flashing in his eyes; the rich, fat patron in his new Mercedes, sweating as he leans on his horn; the bad-tempered minibus drivers cruising like predators.

The heat expands, sucking the air out of the streets to be replaced by the black fumes of the tailgating, beaten-up taxi-vans off which people hang like bunches of grapes. The street hawkers and cripples weave in between the jams. Donkey-carts are bullied through. The shops and stalls and markets spill out, covering every inch of the town. There are, they say, three-quarters of a million points of sale in this vastly expanding city of a million and a half or more people.

Our first call of the day is to Amadou – in whose rooms we are staying – to pay our respects, as we have not seen him yet.

He is a first cousin of Salif's.

We find him sitting behind a wide metal desk in a near-empty office at the back of the Department of Water and Hydraulics workshop. Amadou is a large man with a large, shaven head, a pockmarked face and a glint of humor in his eyes. A Moor in neat Western clothes is standing in front of his desk.

'Tell him it cannot be done,' Amadou is saying to the man, speaking French.

'But you know what they are like,' the Moor replies. 'They insist.'

'They can insist as much as they like, but they know it cannot be done,' Amadou answers back.

At this moment he takes note of our entry and gets up to greet us, dismissing the Moor as he does so with a curt: 'Okay?' He reaches across his desk to shake our hands, and, as the man leaves the room, explains: 'They come to me for favors all the time. This time it's an engineer to go over to their new offices and sort out their well pump. They're management, so they are in charge and can ask what they want, even if it's against the rules, which sending engineers to do private work for them is. Because the new offices are not part of the Département. They're just where they run their little "business" from. Even if I wanted to give them an engineer, I could not spare one now.'

Salif gives a wry smile. 'They're your bosses,' he says. 'You shouldn't antagonize them so.' At this, Amadou breaks out into a deep, rumbling laugh, one that has all the various people hanging around his office grinning broadly. 'They're just businesspeople,' he says. 'They cannot do without me and they know it.'

This is true, as it is well known that Amadou is about the only person in the Département in any position of responsibility who does not treat his job simply as a means of personal gain and who actually knows what he is doing.

There is a constant stream of people stopping by to ask his advice on technical matters, to get him to make orders, to book jobs.

In the early days, he had run the family's irrigation project, the one I had helped Salif set up. He was not long back from Russia at the time, where he had studied engineering, and he had nothing else to do. He was exemplary at the technical side of the job, managing to squeeze a rice yield out of the land no-one had ever attained locally before. But he found dealing with the family frustrating.

'They never leave me enough to invest for the next year,' he told me. 'They are like locusts. They eat everything up.'

We do not stay with Amadou long, just long enough to have a glass of tea brewed by the tea 'boy' who resides on the floor in a corner of the office. Then we are off to Monsieur Adrosso, our 'fix-it' man, whose agricultural machinery shop is not far away.

I have known Monsieur Adrosso for a number of years, during which he has provided us with a quantity of water pumps and other such agricultural hardware. An old Africa hand, he came out to West Africa from Italy as a young man in the late 1950s working for an engineering firm and has stayed on ever since. Now over 70 years old, thin as a rake with yellowing skin, he runs an agricultural import company. He greets Salif and me in his showroom as though we were long-lost friends.

'Ah, ah!' he exclaims ecstatically, 'Messieurs Peter and Salif. Why did you not come to see me earlier? When did you arrive? It is good to see you.' He breaks into a bout of serious-sounding coughing. 'God, it's terrible,' he splutters between breaths.

When he has finished, I ask him about his heart, as the last time I was here he was due to go off to Italy to have surgery on it. He is a heavy smoker.

'My heart? It's not a problem,' he says, dismissing the question with a wave of his arm. 'Come, come into my office.' We leave the showroom, which, like the majority of agricultural and vehicle dealerships in town, is empty, and enter his office. Here, Monsieur Adrosso quickly seats himself behind his desk before opening a drawer and taking out a cigarette. He lights up and is immediately wracked by another bout of coughing. When this is finished, he leans back breathlessly and asks how he can help us.

Dealing with Monsieur Adrosso, I have discovered over the years, is a bit like fishing: there is a certain amount of play involved, and you are never quite sure what you are going to get. On the one hand this can be troublesome; on the other Monsieur Adrosso has provided us over the years with a number of invaluable services.

'Do you know anyone in Customs?' was one of the questions he asked me when Salif first took me to see him. 'No,' he continued, 'but I do. In fact, the Chief of Customs is my great friend. Do you know how good a friend he is?' – Monsieur Adrosso uses the interrogative a lot – 'He is such a good friend I can ring him at any time, like now, see,' he said, picking up the telephone on his desk and dialling a number, 'I am calling him now.' A silence ensued as he waited for the connection, then: 'Ah, Said, it is I, Adrosso. Yes, yes, all well thank you... and you and the family... yes, yes, good... yes, the commission was paid on that last shipment... yes, good. Look, listen Said, I have an English friend here, an Englishman, yes... we will be importing some Lister Pumps... the usual system, eh. Twenty per cent flat, that's right. Good, good. OK, Said, I must go now, OK, bye...' 'There,' Monsieur Adrosso said, replacing the receiver, 'that was him. You heard, didn't you? A flat 20-percent import duty. You could be charged as much as 100 per cent, you know. But we have an understanding. That's how things are done here, you know. Little arrangements, little arrangements.' He chuckled merrily.

In addition to reducing import costs, however, the most invaluable service Monsieur Adrosso provides is simply carrying out his function of importing agricultural machinery: actually producing the goods for us at acceptable prices. All the other importers in town, most of whom we have at one time or another visited, seem as indifferent to our offers of business as are the many vehicle dealerships we have also been to in order to ask about a replacement for our Toyota.

Knowing I can count on Monsieur Adrosso for an opinion on any such matter, and in order to try to clear up my ongoing confusion about why this should be, I now ask him what he thinks about the dealerships' apparent lack of interest in doing any business with us. He looks at me sadly, as though I have a lot to learn.

'What you must understand, Monsieur Peter,' he says, 'is that there is no real agri-industry in this country. There are only peasant farmers and businesspeople. The peasants cannot afford modern machinery and the businesspeople are interested only in quick returns. You will hardly find a single heavy machinery importer here with any stock, agricultural or otherwise. Why is this, you ask? Because the only business they are interested in is the one of making large deals with government or international companies, deals such as supplying 150 water pumps for some state-funded agricultural initiative which they will source from Morocco, getting reconditioned ones made to look new which will break down after a year; or producing two dozen top-of-the range models for a foreign government or corporation wishing to set up a French bean scheme on some newly acquired land that in a few years' time will be abandoned because it is exhausted. You understand,' he continues, 'people here are traders by nature: they want goods in the door one day and out the next. No-one is interested in long-term investment; no-one is interested in developing a genuine agri-industry –

or any other industry for that matter. Why should they be? They are doing quite well as things are.'

This has all been delivered to me in the rapid, highly stylized French unique to Monsieur Adrosso which I can only just follow and which is responsible for the only partial state of comprehension that exists between us. Generally, this does not affect our relationship but, when it comes to more technical matters, it can cause problems. Indeed, so convoluted can our arrangements with him at times become, involving 'proformas', 'bids', 'mid-sea allowances', 'customs rebates', 'forecourt and full set-up differential percentages', that it is not surprising we have occasionally ended up with the wrong piece of equipment. This most recently and most disconcertingly occurred with the purchase of a rice de-husking machine. It is primarily about this that Salif and I have come to see him.

'The rice de-husker...' Salif, who is keen to get down to business, now intercedes.

'Ahhh... yes, yes, yes. The rice de-husker,' Monsieur Adrosso muses for a moment, then continues: 'Monsieur Salif, how many times do I have to tell you? You only have to adjust pressure on the control rack to get the husk out of the reject flue.' He waves his finger at him like a headteacher, then turns to me. 'They never listen,' he says. 'It doesn't matter how many times I tell them, they never listen.'

I glance over to Salif to see whether he is put out by Monsieur Adrosso's patronizing manner, but he is smiling. He knows, as I do, not to take Monsieur Adrosso too seriously. He now takes it on himself to explain the situation again. The fact is that we have had a number of people look at the machine, including Monsieur Adrosso's own mechanic, and it is obvious that we have not received the one we ordered, since this one is specifically adapted to produce little or no chaff, grinding the rice husks to dust instead of leaving them whole for use as livestock feed.

'The husk comes out of the reject flue okay, Monsieur

Adrosso,' Salif says patiently, 'but it is ground to a powder whichever setting you have the rack pressure on. Your mechanic told us himself that it can only be fixed by removing the rack altogether and replacing it with a different one.'

Monsieur Adrosso is waving his hand and shaking his head. 'No, no, no,' he says. Again he turns to me, as if imploring my sympathy. 'They just do not understand machinery,' he says. 'I tell you: there are no more than two or three people in this whole country who understand machines properly, and I'm one of them. But I'll tell you what I'll do, Monsieur Salif,' he says, addressing him again. 'I'll send my mechanic out to you again and make sure this time he knows what to do. OK?' he says, smiling.

The rice de-husker was an expensive piece of machinery that, along with helping farmers make their rice more marketable, was supposed to produce an income to pay some of the running costs of Salif's small development group. It has already been sitting idle for a year and a half. For me, this represents a failure and it is frustrating. 'What about getting a new rack?' I ask.

Monsieur Adrosso grabs a pile of specification manuals nearby and flips pointedly through them. 'See,' he says, 'this rack you talk of doesn't exist. I cannot find it. It doesn't exist.'

I look at Salif to see his reaction. It seems he does not think there is much choice left to him.

'Okay, Adrosso,' he says. 'Send your man.'

We do not stay long after this, just long enough to take a glass of tea. I had wanted to ask Monsieur Adrosso about prices for new Toyotas but Salif has made it clear he would rather I didn't. When it's time to leave, Monsieur Adrosso shakes our hands with enthusiasm and extracts a promise from us that, on our return to the capital to catch my flight out, we will come and have dinner with him. 'I will cook something extra special for you,' he says, smacking his lips. 'King prawns deep fried in batter. And some nice wine. But not for you,' he says, wagging his finger playfully at Salif. 'For you, only orange juice.'

Outside: searing sunlight and heat like a furnace. Amadou Tall is waiting patiently beside the Toyota. I drink deeply from the water bottle that has not left my side all morning. It is March, the end of the 'cool' season, and the temperature must be at least 100 degrees.

We set out on a trail around town looking for an injection pump for the Toyota, which now requires a push each time to start. This involves calling in at a number of spare-part dealers, visiting a couple of sidewalk garages, picking up a mechanic to take with us to another garage where there is a promise of a pump, breaking down, undergoing temporary mid-street repairs, picking up a garage-boy so entirely blackened from head to foot he looks like a Victorian chimneysweep, and finally ending up in an oil-soaked alleyway where 45 minutes of tinkering and hammering by a team of equally blackened men effects the repair we require. Here I dip, a wave of heat-induced feverishness overcoming me. We leave and cruise through town: past a shanty district, a forest of shiny satellite-dish poles rising above it; past the Presidential Palace snuggled closely up to the banks, the ministries and the military barracks; edging our way through the ever-thickening crowds towards the great Cinquième Market where my friend, Mousa Djeng, has a stall. When we can force our way forward no more, we abandon Amadou Tall and make our way by foot.

The Cinquième Market is a test of endurance. Its size and intensity – the heat and smell, the crush of people, the vast array of colors and sights – can easily give rise to a sense of claustrophobia. But I like it. The intensity draws me out of myself. I now no longer feel ill. I move, as though swimming, through the close-packed crowds. Sweat pours down my face. We come to the market, which is indistinguishable at first from the surrounding streets. I have no idea what area it covers, but inside there is an infinity of alleyways and covered passageways, each lined with stalls, each of which is piled high with merchandise: 5,000 plastic sandals; 200 meters of juju items; an alleyway of butchers' tables, their strings of blackened offal alive with flies.

Mousa Djeng's stall is in a wide, uncovered passageway. Down the middle of the passageway sit two rows of vegetable sellers: women in multi-colored dresses behind piles of okra and yams, cabbage and mushed onion balls. Down the sides are small boutiques, the turbaned owners of which hover in doorways with dusters in their hands, flicking stacks of suitcases or piles of shiny kitchen items. And in between each boutique, pressed up against a small patch of wall, are the undergarment sellers. One of these is Mousa Djeng. Like the others, his stall is tiny, consisting of only a small table on which are displayed his wares: underpants, handkerchiefs, vests, bras.

Mousa Djeng is Salif's brother-in-law. He is a farmer from Keniéba, Salif's village, and has sat in this market now for 12 years. Every day, every week, every month for 12 years he has sat in this passageway from early morning till dusk with its press of constantly passing humanity. Never anywhere have I experienced such temperatures as there are in this passageway. Open to the sunlight and closely hemmed in on all sides, the heat is like a hammer blow. I cannot imagine what it must be like in the summer months. And Mousa Djeng has no shade. He sits each day, the direct sunlight bouncing off his forehead. And all this for the most meagre of rewards, as not only does he have to pay rent to the boutique owner whose side wall he uses, but he also must pay both an official market rent and the bribe required by the market authority to allow him to continue occupying his 'illegal' spot. I often wonder just how on earth he survives. He has both a wife and children to support.

It is not these facts, however, that draw me to Mousa Djeng.

What has always made him so special and inspirational to me is simply the look on his face. For Mousa Djeng, whose pale, triangular face is almost oriental in its conformity, has – one can see from the quickest of glances – a compassion and humanity that is exceptional.

He rises from his stool as we approach. 'Monsieur Peter! Salif!' he exclaims, his face lit up. He offers me his seat and pulls another over from a neighboring stallholder for Salif. I see that he does not look well, his face puffy, with a yellowish tinge. Probably jaundice, a common ailment, I reflect. He has not looked well for a number of years.

Most of the other undergarment stallholders in the immediate vicinity are also from Keniéba. This is a little, urban outpost of the village. Mostly, they are young men. Some of them have stalls like Mousa Djeng, others have not graduated to that level of commerce yet and still carry their wares about with them. Everyone looks weary, but there is a palpable sense of camaraderie. Mousa Djeng introduces me to everyone, knowing full well, even though I have met many of them before, that I will not remember their names. He teases them into animation.

'Demba Son... you remember?' he says, a twinkle in his eye. 'You met him in the village fields the year before last... doesn't like to work too hard.' Or, indicating another young man squatting on the ground nearby with a case of wristwatches: 'Ibrahim Tall: a vagabond.' The young man in question smiles mischievously up at us, wagging his finger.

'No, no, no, Djeng,' he says.

I sit with them while Salif goes off in search of someone for whom he has a letter. I ask Mousa Djeng how his business is doing.

'Not so good,' he says, his face momentarily darkening. 'They have put rents up. There is little profit in it now.'

I suggest – half joking, half hopeful he might take up the idea, as it does not look to me as if he can last out here much longer – that perhaps he could go back to the village, take a plot in the irrigation scheme. 'Country life is good for you,' I say.

Mousa Djeng laughs gently. 'It is true. It is true,' is all he says, though.

We sit watching the press of people. As always with marketplaces, I am amazed at how few purchases one actually sees taking place. Now and again, you see someone pick an item up, feel it perhaps, try it against themselves for size, but they never actually seem to clinch a deal.

We are peaceful as we sit, mesmerized by the passing crowds, not feeling the need to converse. Later, when I ask Mousa Djeng whether he has sold anything today, he tells me that he has sold only one vest.

We take our leave when Salif comes back. As we are going, Mousa Djeng presses into my hand three handkerchiefs: a present. I do not want to accept them, especially having just heard that he has only sold one item today, but he will not countenance the slightest objection. 'They are for you... for you,' he repeats with emphasis.

Why is it that, whenever I leave Mousa Djeng, I feel always somehow that I have been blessed?

The sun is low over the town: at its feet the crowds are showing no sign of abating, the traffic at its most chaotic, gridlocking virtually every street. Salif and I pick our way through, stopping off in a street of freezers to see if we can find any reasonable second-hand ones. We do, but they are prohibitively expensive. This is a shame, as I have been wanting to buy a freezer for Salif's wife, Mariam, for a number of years. Electricity finally arrived in Keniéba this year and I know Mariam, who was brought up in a city, finds the summer heat, unrelieved by even as much as a cool drink, difficult.

The traffic and people thin out but we keep walking,

enjoying the soft light and reduced temperature. Later, we stop a taxi and get him to take us back to Amadou's. The serene, quiet district beside the sand dunes where Amadou lives seems a million miles from the madness of the Cinquième.

Evenings at Amadou's can be enlivening or desultory affairs, depending on people's moods. This evening, it seems, will not be enlivening. There are few people around and the inevitable television takes command. Amadou complains of a fever and is quiet most of the time, lying motionless and morose across the carpeted floor, flipping from one anodyne satellite channel to the next. I sit and do various bits of work. Later, we eat fried fish and chips from a large, shared platter, with our left hands. Then I turn in, on my foam mattress in the room that has kindly been put at my disposal.

2 Around Town

An audience with international bankers... The frustrations of the capital... State of the nation... Ramata's story... North Africa's tea ceremony... An Algerian tale

Being Friday, the Muslim holy day, the muezzin down the street is especially keen this morning: the chanting and singing starts at 3.30am and goes on for many hours. By the time I rise at 8.30am, I am exhausted.

We have a rendezvous with an acquaintance of Salif's this morning: Mustapha Demba, who works for one of the large international financial institutions so active and influential in Africa, a man whose brains I want to pick about the development project his organization is funding in the region of the south where we work. When we contacted him yesterday, however, he told us that his office was in the midst of hosting a delegation of the institution's officials who had come to review the project. He could arrange a meeting for us with the head of the delegation, he said.

I have long been aware of this multimillion-dollar project and the massive cynicism directed towards it by anyone who is not directly involved with its implementation and who is not poised to gain financially from it. I want to know if the man with overall responsibility for the project is aware that local people – whether farmers in the target region or ordinary citizens of the capital – regard it as simply another 'gravy train' for those in power. I am fascinated to see whether he is aware of the level of cynicism with which ordinary people in the country regard development projects, especially large, multimillion-dollar ones where the funds and activities are all channelled through local government *départements*.

Mustapha Demba has arranged our meeting for 10.30am, squeezing it into a 10-minute interlude in the visiting delegation's busy schedule.

We find the delegation in a smart hotel in a quiet part of town with which I am not familiar. It is the sort of hotel that can be found anywhere in the world: a building and an atmosphere that seals out any vestiges of the country it is in – five floors of reflective glass and a deep-chilled foyer of marble, clusters of comfy armchairs, piped music and suited businesspeople huddled in corners with well-dressed locals – the club of the élite.

Mustapha Demba meets us out front. He is a friendly, obliging man, always seemingly a little harassed.

'They're running late,' he tells us breathlessly. 'Monsieur Alzane is the program commissioner responsible for the southern development initiative. He will be out soon. It is he who is leading the delegation for whom we are chairing this seminar. I have arranged for you to meet him directly after the round-table fiscal meeting and before he is due to address the delegates in the conference hall. He understands that Salif here is involved in agricultural development in the region and is very keen to meet him. Unfortunately, you will only have a few minutes as we are already behind schedule.'

We take seats in a vacant cluster of armchairs and await developments. The hotel foyer is large and permeated by an air of calm. In town, there may be heat and dust and urban mayhem, but here people drift about as though remote-controlled; whispers of conversations float across the space like flurries of autumn leaves. Salif looks relaxed. Then suddenly there is a hum of commotion at a door beside the expansive reception desk. People are spilling out of a meeting room: a swirl of bobos and suits, animated faces and clasped hands. I see Mustapha Demba, his face shiny, smiling and laughing in a group. Then he is steering the group in our direction: three men, two in suits, one wearing a white bobo almost as immaculate as Salif's. They join us and Monsieur Alzane, a Tunisian, is introduced to us. He is a compact, middle-aged man with an engaging smile. The two other men are introduced as the assistant program commissioner – a tall American – and the regional program facilitator, a smartly dressed Moor who eyes us suspiciously.

The meeting, as promised, is brief. At first there is a little awkwardness, as it is unclear who should take the lead. Eventually Salif is persuaded to do so. He explains the work we are involved in, and then Monsieur Alzane, taking the initiative, questions him closely on many details. The American chips in with a few polite queries. The regional program facilitator remains silent. Time is already nearly out and Monsieur Alzane, now shaking Salif's hand, is tying up with: 'It has been very interesting to meet you. We are here for no other purpose than to help develop agriculture in your region. It is of vital importance that local people are included in this process, and I hope you will make yourself known to the Project Office. Our regional program officer here,' he says, smiling at the Moor, 'will, I'm sure, be happy to meet with you.' The man in question looks anything but enthralled.

I have not yet managed to say much but take the opportunity as the meeting breaks up to address Monsieur Alzane a little to the side. I am not sure how to start and so simply say that people in the south are very skeptical about the ability of the project to deliver any results.

'They do not trust those responsible for implementing the project,' I say.

Monsieur Alzane fixes me with a look of great earnestness. 'That is true,' he says. 'And it is not surprising, as there have been many mistakes in the past. But that is one of the primary objectives of this project: to develop effective delivery systems and restore confidence. What we need is good people, men like your friend here. Send him to us. It is people like him we need.'

I tell him that I will ask him and mention that I have spoken to farmers in the south who say the project benefits are not reaching them.

Monsieur Alzane stays focused. 'It is still early days,' he says. 'Much has changed with us over the last few years and we have introduced new practices. Tell your friend to have confidence in us. It is not easy, but we are doing things differently this time.' Mustapha Demba is at our elbows now, and it is time for Monsieur Alzane to go. With a brief nod of his head, he is off. The assistant program commissioner, the American, politely shakes both my and Salif's hands, but the regional program manager – the 'minder' – is already halfway across the foyer.

Outside, Salif and I decide to walk for a while. We send Amadou Tall ahead to await us at the house of a friend of Salif's whom we wish to visit. The streets here are paved and relatively free of traffic, and, as we walk, we talk. We are strangely inspired by the meeting, perhaps because it brings into focus how simple and effective the work we do is when compared with the Machiavellian complications of doing development work at the level of large international institutions. Salif was impressed by Monsieur Alzane. It was difficult not to be. His charm and natural authority were infectious. I ask Salif if he thinks things might be different this time, but his response is short: 'No.'

'Why not?' I ask

'Because things never change here,' he replies.

'Why not?' I repeat.

'Because it is always the same men in charge. There are too many *interests* for there to be any change. Even the President has little control.'

'But there is much development in Nouakchott,' I say, playing devil's advocate. 'There are buildings going up everywhere. I even heard they are building two new Sheraton Hotels.' And indeed this is true: Nouakchott is on a vast growth spurt, with new districts, shiny banks and market arcades appearing as though overnight. There is money about – of this there is no doubt.

Salif smiles.

'The hotels! Yes, it is true,' he says. 'But it does not mean much. It is all private money. Nothing is done for the city or the poor.'

Again, this is true. There is a free-for-all here, as everyone knows, with the country's resources – fish, iron ore, oil, land – being sold off to the highest bidder by the clan-based Moorish business cartels who, in cahoots with the military, vie with each other for control of the country. A top five per cent garner large sums, some of which they might at least now invest in their own country – not an occurrence that would have taken place only a few years ago. But, as Monsieur Adrosso pointed out the day before, they do not invest in anything as fiddly as industry or other long-term investments, preferring the hothouse of the property market or other such quick-money returns. The city may indeed be booming in one sense – and the vast amounts of vehicles visible and goods for sale indicate at least some sort of trickle-down – but there is almost zero municipal spending, presumably because the few taxes that are collected are not prioritized for such things as drainage systems, roads, sewers or traffic control.

The city, indeed, is a dump: even those areas that might by some stretch of the imagination be termed middle-class,

where hectares of large whitewashed, concrete buildings have sprung up, are surrounded by nothing but a wasteland of sand, refuse, dead animals and, anywhere near the rainy season, fetid pools of water. Indeed, for three weeks during the rainy season last year much of the entire city was under a foot of sewer-filled water. Other than in the fortified compounds of the foreign embassies, there are no parks in the capital; indeed, again, outside the quartiers of the rich and their foreign backers, there is barely a single tree at all. All in the city is private. The poor majority live off the scraps in their vast shanties of squalor: ignored, subjugated, controlled. There are no revolutions taking place here. As Salif said, even the President has little control.

I ask Salif whether he thinks Monsieur Alzane – as implicated as he and his institution assuredly are with the regime that controls the country – is himself personally honest; whether he actually believes that the huge investment his institution is making in the south will not, in the traditional manner, simply be frittered away in a labyrinthine bureaucratic process designed to line the pockets of the élite. Salif is unsure.

'Most people believe in what they are doing,' he says. And it is true. Monsieur Alzane no doubt believes that he and his institution can bring about change here. But the truth is, it is not in the interest of those who are benefiting from this change to look too deeply into the direction in which it is going. In a couple of years' time Monsieur Alzane will be moved on to another job and what goes on here then will no longer be his concern. That is the reality.

We are two cynics, Salif and I: crabby and indignant, perhaps, but also incensed at what we learn and see. It is always like this in the capital: complicated, frustrating. Once we are out in the countryside with the farmers, everything becomes simpler.

Midday, and the sun is directly overhead, all color bleached from our surroundings. By the time we reach the dusty backstreet in the busy, commercial part of town where Salif's friend, Sheik, has his compound, I am gritting my teeth and forcing my feet to carry me forwards. We enter a rusty metal door, and Salif calls out a greeting. In a moment Sheik's wife appears, a tall, slim lady who greets us warmly and directs us across the small compound to the lounge.

The lounge is a simple room, comfortable with gaudy-colored divans lining the walls, purple carpeting and, at the far end, a glass-fronted cabinet, empty save for a few Arabic books and a plastic football trophy. In a corner on a small table is a computer with a cloth draped over it. Although the room feels spacious, it is not particularly large and suffers the disadvantage of having a corrugated-iron roof, the heated metal of which creates furnace-like conditions. Regardless, we collapse into the divans, and shortly Sheik appears.

Sheik is an old colleague of Salif's from the days when they worked for the national mining company in the north. An older man of Moorish extraction, he is tall and thin, with wild grey hair and the air of a disorientated professor. He peers at us over his spectacles and greets us profusely, holding my hands for an extended period, repeating: 'Ah, Peter, Peter... Ah, Peter...' as though he were giving himself time to catch up with the speed of events. He has obviously just woken up.

Sheik teaches economics at a college nearby and is, by his own description, 'a minor intellectual'. He also owns a small copy shop and takes in lodgers in order to supplement an income that is patently inadequate. His passion is politics, and he is a leading figure in one of the many small opposition parties, many of which were banned for years.

Salif and I have been visiting Sheik for a number of years and the first thing that always occurs is the protracted business of providing each of us with a drink. There are choices. Often we go for the easier option of sodas, the bottles of which are fetched from a nearby boutique by any easily locatable local boy or, if they are available, one of his student lodgers. His wife is never implicated in these proceedings. Once the bottles of Coke or Fanta have appeared, glasses must then be found and washed out, a small tray on which to serve them produced, and drinks poured ceremoniously. Sheik conducts all these proceedings with a firm but gracious authority, rolling up his sleeves to do the pouring himself. When he insists we go for the more complex alternative of home-mixed powdered milk or hibiscus drink, however, considerable amounts of time can elapse, because these require many implements and ingredients – water, sugar, blocks of ice, jugs, whisks, glasses and spoons – few of which are ever readily available. However, once all is completed and Sheik has mixed and stirred and tested to his satisfaction, we sit back and relax.

Conversations at Sheik's, not surprisingly, quickly turn political. But this is no man of seething sedition, filled with embittered ideology. Sheik's gradual downward trajectory, from a high point of influence in some earlier government, has been conducted with grace and objectivity. He views the current political situation as no more than farcical and his modest personal circumstances as merely unfortunate. When I mention our recent meeting with Monsieur Alzane and the institution for which he works, he is eloquent.

'That institution has been here for 30 years,' he says. 'Three years ago, they gave $22.5 million for a major municipal infrastructure program. Already, during the planning phase, $14 million, two-thirds of the total, have been *gorged*,' – this last word emphasized with great élan – 'and the remaining $8.5 million are in the process of being massacred. Then, at the beginning of last year, a delegation from the institution came here to see the progress of the project and, in their own words, as reported in the press, went away "well pleased with all they had seen". The whole nation was astounded… a-s-t-o-u-n-d-e-d, I tell you,' he repeats, enunciating the word, his face lit up with the sheer, beautiful incredulity of it.

'This country is in a mess,' he goes on. 'It is like this across much of Africa. The resource boom is producing growth rates in many countries that are impressive – very impressive. And in some countries there may even be some proper development – and by this I mean the development of good governance, of jobs and manufacturing and industry – but for most, and certainly for us here, it means only a short-term feast that puts wealth and power in the hands of people in whose interest it is to subjugate their populations. This sort of development leads only to greater poverty and divide, even to civil war: consequences naturally that are enabled and abetted by those who wish to invest in such places. Not that we have got to that here yet, thanks be to Allah; not that we are incapable of it…' and on he continues for a while, shaking his head and twinkling his eyes long after his French has lost me. But I get the drift. On the subject of state higher education, which comes up a little later, he is equally eloquent.

'The university here is weak – practically non-existent,' he says disapprovingly. 'Those who finish their third year and wish to go on for a masters – and anything less than a masters is worthless here – find it practically impossible without private wealth, as they must go abroad and state grants are very few. And anyway, there are few jobs here for graduates now as the civil service is filled with businesspeople... businesspeople, I ask you. Those who get the very best grades...' he continues, but gets no further as at this moment his wife pops her head in the door and asks if we will partake of the midday meal. We thank her but say that we can't as we promised yesterday that we would take it with Mousa Djeng.

Sheik does not resume his theme when his wife has gone. Instead, he remains staring at the floor for a while, nodding, a seraphic smile spread across his face. Presently, the mood passes and he looks up.

'Tell me of Ramata,' he says to Salif. 'How is Ramata?'

Ramata is Salif's eldest child whom I have known since she was young, the neat, prettily presented child I had seen in the bush taxi all those years ago. Now 25 and living on the outskirts of Paris, she was at one time one of Sheik's student lodgers. Salif looks uncomfortable.

'Ramata is well,' he replies.

'She is married?' Sheik prompts.

'Yes. She is married... to a Senegalese.'

Ramata is a bright, attractive young lady but her story troubles Salif. Salif is a traditional man in as much as he believes in values such as family, respect and filial duty. He has always treated his seven children, and especially the boys, with great – if clearly loving – firmness. These values, however, do not encompass all that is traditional and in many ways Salif is also a modern man. He despises tribalism and all that it does to undermine so much in Africa, he is non-racist, and he is a hands-on father in a way unusual in Africa.

As a result, when it came to Ramata's education, because she showed promise, it did not occur to him for a minute not to spend heavily just because she was a girl. So Ramata, having successfully passed through local primary and secondary schools, came to the capital to attend college.

It took her five years to pass her baccalaureate, or bac, and this was not because she was less academically able in any way, but because, for two years in a row, the results of the exam were so undermined by wealthy parents paying for good results for their offspring that the international baccalaureate board nullified all results in the country. This was a hard time for Ramata as it meant that she had to prepare for and take the exams three years in a row – not that her distress was ever apparent, for she maintained into adulthood the same serene composure that she always had as a child. Each time we came to Sheik's, she would appear, with immaculate manners, looking as serene and well presented as a model on a catwalk.

All this time, of course, Salif was paying not only for her education, which was only partially state-funded, but also for her lodgings and living. And then, when she did finally pass her exams, she had to wait a whole further year for her application for a university grant to be processed, only to hear that, despite having passed the bac in the top 10 per cent, no grant was available for her. With a little help from me, Salif somehow now managed to rustle up enough money not only for a passport, visa and air ticket but also for the fees to study computing at a small university in France. After a year, Ramata was earning enough by working in a fast-food restaurant in the evenings to pay for her own living expenses; after two years, she was covering some of her own tuition fees as well. After her third year, she was only attending college part-time and had a full-time job and resident's permit. She was now financially independent of Salif, and it was only some 12 months ago that she announced she was going to marry a young Senegalese man she had met in France. This came as a shock to Salif and put his 'modernity' to the test, for not only were the young man and his family completely unknown to him, but also his permission for the marriage had not been sought.

For all Salif's disdain of tribalism, the fact is that the Senegalese man is a Wolof, not a Peul, and Salif would prefer that this was not the case. It is virtually unheard of for people of Salif's background to marry outside their ethnic group. Indeed, it is pretty rare for them to marry outside the extended family, but to marry someone from an entirely different people is exceptional. And for it to be done in such a manner, without any consultation or permission being sought... It does test Salif. He does not like it, but the fact is, he has given his blessing for the marriage, and I think perhaps the greatest sadness he and Mariam, his wife, feel is that it almost certainly means Ramata does not intend ever to come back to Mauritania to live.

Sheik smiles sympathetically at Salif's hesitant reply.

'Ramata... Ramata... Yes, she always did know what she wanted,' he muses. 'A girl who knew where she was going.'

Sheik sees us to the door of his compound when we leave. Here he clasps my hand. 'You will come back,' he says. 'Yes, yes, you will come back...' But already I can see that he has moved on; his mind is elsewhere. It cannot be easy, I think, being Sheik.

The Toyota is parked across the alleyway. We make our way across town to the populous Cinquième district where Mousa Djeng, with whom we are to pass the afternoon, lives.

Mousa Djeng's home is in one of the old residential buildings that date from the first major expansion of the city after the colonial era, 40-odd years ago. Constructed of brick, the building is substantial and solid and houses two floors of rooms facing an inner courtyard strung with washing. In each room is a family or a group of students or workmates or any combination of those who can scrape together enough to pay the low rent. There is no running water, sporadic electricity, a squad of ducks living on the roof, and only two toilets for the 70 or 80 residents.

Mousa Djeng lives with his wife and five children in a room on the ground floor. For a number of years this is where I used to stay on my visits. It was not easy, as the building was particularly noisy, with babies crying, music blaring and arguments going on all night. The mosquitoes were bad, the room airless and the toilets unpleasant. But what was lost in physical comfort was surpassed in kindness and welcome. Always, clean sheets would be produced, the room would be fumigated against mosquitoes, and when I looked tired in the evening, the room would be cleared of people, Mousa Djeng and his family sleeping with neighbors.

Mousa Djeng's wife, Salif's sister Fatimata, is a woman with that same blend of strength and tenderness of eye I knew in her, and in Salif's mother, all those years before. She produces a traditional midday meal of white rice, vegetables and fish in a large metal bowl around which we all gather to eat. The food is delicious, a stew of fresh catfish, carrots, okra and aubergine ladled over a bed of rice. Mousa Djeng is attentive, depositing juicy morsels of fish he has pulled from the carcass in front of me like offerings. We eat our fill, then, having washed hands, sit back while tea is made.

There are 10 of us present: me, Salif and the ever-present, but mostly silent Amadou Tall; Mousa Djeng, Fatimata, and two of their children; a couple of young men and a young woman I don't know; and Mustapha, a small, skinny cousin of Salif's who is a military nurse at the main hospital in town and who is inclined to attach himself to me whenever I am in town.

Amadou Tall sets about making the tea, performing the same methodical tea ceremony that is not only being repeated in virtually every room in every house in the city, but also in the majority of houses across the Sahara and West Africa. First, he gathers the required ingredients and implements, most of which are to hand: the tea tin, the  two tiny glasses, the small metal teapot. A bowl for slops is produced; so too are fresh mint, a large mug of water and the sugar. A small aluminium brazier with a few pieces of glowing charcoal is brought in. In tens of millions of rooms the same actions are taking place with only minimal variations, depending on the availability of mint, or using bottled gas instead of charcoal, or sugar coming in lumps rather than loose: rich, poor; urban, rural; Moors, southern tribes; in palaces and desert camps; fuel for busy merchants or stimulant for the addicted. The long hot hours of the afternoon, the long empty days of poverty, pass to the metronomic dance of the tea-maker's hands.

Three times the tea is made from the same tea leaves, added to the heated water, stewed, sweetened, tasted and poured from teapot to glass, glass to glass and back to pot again. Once a good head of froth has been produced, and all implements have been rinsed of any stickiness, the glasses, containing an inch of extremely strong, sweet tea beneath the froth, are handed around on the tray, replenished for each new person who is required to drain his or her glass in a succession of quick, noisy sups. These are the bare bones of the operation, but the art and brilliance, the mesmeric play, is in just how elegantly, how apparently effortlessly and how daringly it is carried out. It is true that for some the operation is simply a function, and in fact most, being modest, would profess it to be little else. But the speed and precision that are applied to the mixing process, pouring the tea into the glasses from ever greater heights at ever greater speeds until the hands and the glass and the teapot are barely more than a blur, belie this. The neat, precise manner in which every part of the operation is performed, from managing the charcoal to handling the often red-hot teapot, to measuring the tea and sugar, tell you there is much more to this than just the quenching of thirst. The best practitioners are those who can drag out the production of the three brews all afternoon or evening. And when the short, sweet explosion of hot liquid does eventually burst in your mouth, it feels good and gives a zest to all those long idle hours.

Mustapha, the military nurse, is sitting uncomfortably close to me. To distract him, I prompt him to tell the story of the time he was in Algeria, where he was sent to train in radiography, a story most of us know well but few tire of hearing.

'There were 22 of us sent there,' he says without hesitation. 'We were sent there for different reasons, although I was in the radiology department. At that time the troubles in the country were still bad and when we arrived we were taken from the airport to the city in buses with blacked-out windows. Sometimes at night we would even hear bombs exploding. We were there for two years and were only allowed to leave the military hospital where we worked once in the last week. Only once in two years,' he goes on, giggling a little now, 'were we allowed to leave. And we went to the cinema. But one of our group... one of our group did not like the film we were going to see, so he... he...' he chokes out, his giggles getting the better of him, 'he stayed... stayed back at the hospital.' Everywhere people are chuckling, as they know what is coming. 'He stayed back at the hospital...' Mustapha goes on, 'because... because... because he didn't like the film.' People are rolling around now, Mousa Djeng holding his stomach as though in pain. 'He... he...' Mustapha just manages to blurt out, 'he thought it would be boring.'

It's too much. People are rolling backwards and forwards with laughter, tears streaming down their faces. 'Boring...' Mustapha repeats again, 'too boring.' All those days and years of boredom, all those hours of hardship are forgotten, as though they never were.

We return to Amadou's as the evening is drawing in. Here there is a scene not dissimilar to the one we have just left: a compressed get-together. Amadou is over his fever of the previous evening and is presiding cross-legged before some tea-making implements. Amadou is a meticulous tea maker and conducts the proceedings with all the precision of his engineer's training.

'You're going tomorrow?' he asks Salif as he pours tea from a great height into a glass, guillotining the steaming thread at just the right moment.

'Insh'Allah,' Salif replies: God willing.

Amadou mixes from glass to glass. 'When will you be back?' he asks.

'In about nine days,' Salif says.

'You saw Adrosso today,' he asks, concentrating on his tea making.

'Yesterday,' Salif replies.

'And his mechanic will fix the de-husker?'

'He's going to send him out again,' Salif says.

Amadou chuckles, shaking his head. 'Adrosso. Ha! A joker – a bandit,' he says.

'Perhaps,' Salif replies a little stiffly, 'but we can only do what we can do.'

Amadou abruptly changes his tone. 'Of course,' he says. 'Of course. Surely you will be able to fix the de-husker.' Salif is older than Amadou. He is also head of the family. The respect in which Amadou holds Salif, and his deference to him, however, stem from much more than just this.

3 Road to the South

The sand-dune sea... Incident in a bush taxi... Roadblock savvy... Salif's story... The women's irrigation co-operative... A trip to Casamance... Plea for a dying town... A US company's land grab... Survival in a changing climate... Kaédi – routine disaster zone

We are leaving for Keniéba. This is a journey I have made many times, and little has changed since the earliest days. The main difference now is that the tarmac road, instead of running out as soon as it hits the South, goes all the way to Kaédi, the main regional town. The route is beautiful. Once the last tattered remains of the capital have been shaken off, the road runs true and pure, laid flat like a ribbon over an endless sea of sand dunes. The sand dunes are ranked into a succession of huge swells, like those in an ocean, in between which are long pale valleys. All is golden, the pale gold of the valleys contrasting with the deep gold of the dunes.

Driving down the open road into one of the wide valleys, then speeding up the far side towards the crest of the next range of dunes – with always the added excitement that a vehicle might appear over the blind summit on the wrong side of the road at just the wrong moment – is exhilarating. You can lose yourself and your thoughts far out in the milky sea of sand. The world here is clean and clear, and always I get the urge to call a halt to the vehicle, climb out and embrace all that I can see.

The road is constantly under siege from the dunes, with a squad of huge diggers tasked to keep it clear. Scuttling back and forth like crabs on the seashore, the diggers maneuver each dune, helping it, like an old lady, over the road.

Later, after some 300 kilometers, the dunes peter out and the road, which up to now has been running due east, turns south. Now the land is flat and gravelly: a totally unremarkable but still beautiful plain of grey, in between the empty horizons roamed by the goat-, cattle- and camel-herders. Sometimes the concentrations of livestock are greater, sometimes less, depending on the time of year. Earlier in the year, if the rains have been good, the herders will keep further north, but as the pastures are exhausted, or if the rains have failed, they will move southwards where the grasses are fuller. Some are proud desert people with great herds of camels, their odd, pale, cavernous beasts looking prehistoric as they mill about a waterhole. Most are the poorer Black Moors, the Harratin, who, if they are lucky, will have a handful of thin cattle and a herd of sheep and goats. There are tents and camps and small windblown communities. Then, in the South, where the road once again turns east, pretty Peul and Soninke villages start to

appear: close-knit warrens of dung-smoothed houses from which large, brightly colored mosques rear. This is the true Sahel, where cultures, customs and climates meet, merge and clash.

Until we had our own vehicle this journey was always completed in a share-taxi. The downside of this was that the journey could take as much as 15 hours. The upside was the intimacy and camaraderie that can always be found in share-taxis. Each journey is an adventure. Each one never fails to take you to the limit of your endurance. But before any of this, the taxi-park has first to be negotiated.

Each major destination in the country has its own taxi-park in which the share-taxis queue for customers on a first-come, first-served basis. Anything up to 70 of these Peugeots or Mercedes will be ranked in each taxi-park, with a taxi-park chief and a ticket seller in charge.

I remember the start of one particular journey. As usual, Salif and I arrived at the taxi-park early in the hope of catching the first vehicle, but, as usual, we were not early enough. Already the first Peugeot was fully charged and ready to go. In the second, five of its nine places were already sold. Having ourselves taken a further two, this left only two seats. A further hour passed before these were filled, during which time the ranks of young merchandise sellers with their trays of Chinese goods plied their trade, successfully getting money off Salif for first a comb, then a torch and then a pair of sunglasses. Once it was confirmed that all the tickets were sold, the negotiations as to what was going to go onto the roof and how much it would cost began: two goats in a sack; two sacks of grain; four chickens tied by the feet. With each addition, the vehicle sank lower on its axle. The ticket seller was theatrical. One moment laughing, the next shouting, the next sullen or absent, he played the scene to perfection, rebuffing overtures of conciliation from his hierarchical competitor, the taxi-park chief, pulling items already on the roof off in an apparent fury, only finally accepting a compromise when it became apparent that everyone had had enough.

Once this was over, a standoff took place between two passengers over who should sit in the front – it was significant where you sat in the vehicle, the back row being more cramped than the second row, which was not as good as the front. An older man – a rough country farmer type in a skullcap and coarse tunic – had seated himself on the window side of the front passenger seat; an elderly lady already occupied the other half of the seat. There he sat, a look of wooden determination on his face, ignoring the ticket seller. 'Monsieur,' the ticket seller kept repeating, 'you must get up and vacate this place. It has already been reserved.' A businessman with a briefcase and a safari suit stood glowering nearby.

The man in the vehicle continued to stare determinedly ahead of him.

'I said: Monsieur, you must give up this seat,' the ticket seller repeated.

'Why should I give up the seat?' the man snapped.

'Because this Monsieur here reserved it when he bought his ticket.'

'There was nothing reserving the seat when I took it,' the man replied, returning his gaze to the middle distance and ignoring anything more that was said. The ticket seller, a man who knew when he had met his match, closed the door and turned back to the businessman. 'You had better take a place in the back,' he said.

The businessman, however, was incensed. Stepping forward and tapping loudly on the vehicle window, he snapped: 'Vacate your seat, Monsieur. You are holding up the vehicle. What are you? Are you a fool? I reserved the seat. It is not your place.'

The man stared stonily before him, ignoring him.

'Is he a fool? What is he doing?' the businessman, furious

now, complained to those around, then turned back to the ticket seller and demanded to see the taxi-park chief. The chief was nowhere to be found just then, however, so he stalked off to a nearby tea stall where he sat huffily down on a bench.

The rest of the passengers were patient. The situation was absurd, and they discussed it, half laughingly, with each other and with any number of bystanders. Attempts were made to persuade either party to back down. Neither would countenance it, the man in the vehicle mulishly ignoring all suggestions, the businessman too angry now to compromise. It was suggested that the elderly lady in the other half of the seat should be moved to the middle row so that both men could sit in the front, but she was infirm and it had taken some considerable difficulty to get her there in the first place. The impasse continued, then the taxi-park chief appeared.

'Why hasn't this vehicle gone?' he shouted, imposing himself on the scene; then, once he was filled in, continued wildly: 'It should be gone. It's blocking the way. Where's the driver? Get him to move it out of the way.' The driver, however, had gone off with a shrug some time earlier. The chief was angry. He pulled the taxi door open and shouted at the man.

'What are you doing? I will call the police. Get out now.'

He made a half-hearted attempt to pull the man out, which the man fended off like a flustered stork. 'Don't touch me,' he yelped.

'Take his bags off the roof,' the taxi-park chief cried. 'Take them off.' No-one moved to obey him, so he marched off, saying he would fetch the police.

Time was passing, and a crowd had gathered. It was obvious that pride was now at stake. I would not perhaps have remembered this incident were it not for the fact that it was Salif who sorted it out. You could see that the man in the taxi – a country fellow who might never have been to the city before – felt threatened and confused by his surroundings. He did not want to be 'shown up'. Speaking gently, with infinite patience, and addressing him as he would an elder, Salif asked simply that the man take a place in the back so that we could all begin our long journey. This was enough. The deference and respect in Salif's tone was genuine, and it brought the man out of himself. With no more ado he simply climbed out and took his place in the back.

It is Friday, the Muslim holy day, and the city is busy as we head out of town for our destination in the south. There are parliamentary and council elections due shortly in the country and, all along the side of the roads, we pass large billboards advertising parties and their candidates. There are a few women among these, but the majority are men, all wearing dark business suits, and all are of Moorish extraction. Their slogans unanimously trumpet that new, shiny buzzword: transparency.

It is the beginning of the weekend and the *patrons* or bosses are off out of town to their country retreats. These will be well-decked-out tents where dependants and retainers will be waiting with herds of camels specially brought in so that the *patron* and his guests can have fresh camel's milk. They bomb past us in the smartest of overland vehicles. Wheezing lorries struggle up the hills of dunes like old men, billowing out black smoke, colorful tribes of people perched atop their laden backs. Open-backed Toyota Landcruisers – the favored means of transport for true desert folk, with water *guerbas* slung camel-style from their sides and netting holding down the baggage in their backs – stream past, a hunch of turbaned men straining into the wind above their cabs. Occasionally, we pass large articulated trucks coming in the other direction, laden to double their height with hay or wood or sacks of charcoal. These are the true 'ships of the desert', rumbling out across the plains, from country to country, from south to north and east to west, linking ports and markets, bringing the plastic items of the outside world in, transporting 10,000 calabashes.

As we progress, the traffic thins until, after some hours, for much of the time we have the road to ourselves. Amadou Tall drives cautiously: we cannot anyway go very fast. He is adept at managing the many roadblocks where police or military or sometimes customs officers check the legality of vehicles, people or goods, often in competition with each other. Smart vehicles, those obviously owned by *patrons*, simply cruise slowly straight through the blocks, a friendly wave perhaps to the police or customs officers. Amadou Tall, too, likes to try this, only he knows that in our half-wrecked vehicle we are by no means guaranteed success. Each block is a gamble. Slowing down too much as we approach shows a lack of confidence; on the other hand, vehicles are supposed to come to a complete standstill a hundred meters off the roadblock before approaching at walking pace. This means he risks censure if he comes too fast and lack of credibility if he goes too slow. But Amadou Tall was not a truck driver for nothing. He knows how to gauge each block. Sometimes he will pull up and, if requested, we will dutifully present our IDs; at others he cruises right on through. Only occasionally does he get it wrong. Amadou Tall can be tough, though, and negotiates fiercely against any 'fines' the police or soldiers wish to impose. For him, it's all in a day's work.

These days, the only occasion such 'rules' of the road do not apply is when encountering the new militaristic police force, created recently to shore up the regime's control – a disciplined and well-armed cohort of stern-faced young men who can appear suddenly and anywhere. No-one – *patrons*, ordinary people, even the regular police – messes with them, for they do not know the meaning of 'negotiation'.

We drive for four hours, which brings us to Boutilimit, the first and only town we encounter before we reach the South. The place is a hive of commerce spread out in a wide sand

valley and concentrated on the road that passes through its midst. Turbaned men; sharp, desert faces; haggling; piles and mounds of merchandise; donkey-carts struggling under massive loads; laughter, shouts; the smell of dust and spice: we push our way down the road, which has become a market for the crowd of merchants who seemingly need only to move goods from one side of it to the other to make a profit. Here there are many restaurants: open-sided tents with mats on the ground where tea and food is served. We are keen for a stop here, as after four hours we need a break. We stagger into one of the restaurants. Here Salif orders tea and roasted meat. It's sweaty and the sunlight outside the shade of the tent is a blinding white. A few other travellers are flopped down on the grubby mats on which flies are scattered like currants. Nearby, the meat roaster grins under his turban as he stands sweating before his blackened burner. A tea boy is working at a succession of teapots. A large woman with a grubby infant playing in the dust by her side presides over a cauldron of rice, doling ladlefuls onto platters onto which a few pieces of gristle in a sauce are added. People share their platters, insisting that complete strangers join them, as no-one likes to eat alone: it just does not feel right.

It was here in this town at one of these roadside restaurants that, many years ago, Salif first told me something of his background.

He was born in a herders' camp in the bush, not far from Keniéba, he told me. His family was traditionally of the teacher/holy-man caste. In those days, though, he said, life was not as it is now. Even small families had cattle herds 200 strong. Thousand-strong herds were not uncommon. The countryside, he said, was so well forested then that you could travel half a day barely leaving the shade of the trees – now, of course, most of the trees have either died or been cut for firewood. The rains were more dependable then, he said, and people had plenty to eat.

People were proud and strong then, fattened on cow's milk and the couscous they made from their rain-fed millet. Not that life was without difficulty. People had to work hard, but they were proud and had surplus food to take them through the bad years.

Of his six siblings, Salif was the one chosen to be educated. From the age of eight he was sent to Keniéba to attend both primary and Qur'anic schools. This did not excuse him from family chores, however, and every day he would have to walk the 15 kilometers there and back, helping out with the sheep and goats when he got home. It was not easy. At weekends, he said, he would be out with them in the bush. Herding the sheep and goats was the job of the boys. From the earliest of ages, he and his brothers were charged with taking them out for the day to graze. Often, they'd be out from dawn to dusk, the long hot day relieved only by the water container they carried and perhaps a roasted corncob. One day, when he was about six, Salif got lost.

'It was nearing dusk and my brothers and I were heading home when one of the goats became separated from the rest,' he said. 'I went after it, not expecting to have any difficulty in bringing it back. But, for some reason, the animal seemed determined to get itself lost and soon I was fighting my way through an area of thick scrub. I was too far from my brothers to alert them now, and anyway I still thought that at any moment I would catch up with the goat. On I went, always sure I would soon catch the beast, chasing after it as the dusk thickened. Gradually, however, it became harder to see and soon I lost track of the beast altogether. I decided to turn back but was unsure now of the direction and went the wrong way.'

'It was not long before I was lost,' Salif continued. 'When night fell I did not know what to do so I lay down on the sand and slept. The next day at dawn my father found me. They had been looking all night.'

Salif was exceptionally bright and not only did well at primary school, passing the exams to enter the Lycée in Kaédi, but from there he made it on to, first, college in the capital, and then, having passed his baccalaureate with good grades, further education in the south of France. There he studied bookkeeping and accountancy for a placement with the national mining company. He lived and worked in the north of Mauritania at the mining company for 18 years. In that time, five of his surviving six children were born, but during the whole period he was never once put up for promotion. People he had arrived with from college moved on up the hierarchy, some even becoming directors. Many, many others, arriving long after him, also passed on up. Being a Black African from the South, he was effectively barred from promotion. In the end, he'd had enough and he requested early retirement. This was a vital point. If his request was accepted, it meant he would be paid his retirement entitlement, which he could use to set himself up in business back home. If his request was rejected, he would have to resign, meaning he would get nothing. 'For a year and a half my application sat in an in-tray,' Salif said. 'In the end, they gave me nothing. I worked for them for 18 years and I got nothing.'

The noise of the wind and its desiccated, blow-dryer heat coming in through the Toyota's open window is exhausting and it comes almost as something of a relief when, later in the day, we break down: silence; the condensed heat of mid-afternoon; a patch of virgin desert, ours for the while.

It's the starter-motor, of course. The 'new' one is no good. Amadou Tall is unfazed. He tinkers about the engine. We peer in with suggestions. We try the ignition. Nothing. Time passes. At no moment does Salif or Amadou Tall look concerned. I am, though. Even if we manage to get the vehicle going now – and I'm quite sure we will, as when did I ever fail to make it to my destination when travelling in Africa? – we have a lot to accomplish over the next 10 days, and I do not think this vehicle is going to manage for us. The day after tomorrow we have our development consultant arriving to lead the two-day seminar. I do not want to be transporting him on a donkey-cart.

The vehicle coughs into life and we clamber in.

Villages and small towns are more frequent now. Most of them are unprepossessing collections of cement and mud buildings scattered like abandoned bricks on the empty plains. One of these is Danodine, where we stop off as Salif wishes to see a solar-powered irrigation project we have heard about, run by a women's co-operative.

Danodine looks deserted as we approach it over the plain. We find a solitary old man wrapped in his turban against the wind in one of the wide, wind-driven spaces that seem to make up most of the town. We draw up beside him.

'Where is everybody?' we ask, having first greeted him with the ritualistic enquiries after health and well-being of family.

The old man points to the south. 'At the gardens,' he says.

We head on and soon see some movement in the heat haze in a depression beyond the edge of town. The movement turns into a dash of color, which in turn becomes a crowd of women working in an area of fenced-in vegetable plots. Nearby is a bank of eight solar panels and a well.

The women greet us but are busy about their work, carrying water to and from a large cistern. They are playful and smile and giggle at us but do not stop. We ask for the president of the co-operative and before long a tall, shy-looking woman with watery eyes appears. We greet her politely and Salif asks her some questions: how does the system work? Who installed it?

The solar panels, Salif tells me, are connected to a pump 25 meters down in the well, which sends water up a pipe and fills the cistern from which the women are watering their plots. There are 200 women in the co-operative, and they work one hectare in all. The solar panels and pump have been provided and installed by a national agency, paid for, the woman says, by 'foreigners'. Two women have been trained to turn the pump on and off twice a day and to dust the solar panels.

Salif asks the president whether they've had any problems and she points to a group of women on the far side of the co-operative's enclosure, drawing water in the traditional manner from another well. 'They do not want to participate in the solar project,' she says.

'Why not?' I ask.

The woman shrugs. 'They say they were not told about it.'

'Can't they join in now?'

'They say there's never enough water,' she replies.

I can see this is going to take some untangling. Further conversation reveals that the women who come earliest to the gardens tend to use up all the water, leaving nothing for those who come later. This cannot be resolved by leaving the pump on for longer because after four hours the well begins to get low and requires the rest of the day to replenish itself. This is not the main problem, though. The main problem, according to a man who has just appeared beside us and who now politely intercedes, is that the other women do not pay the co-operative stipend.

'All the members must pay a stipend,' the man explains, 'which is used by the co-operative to cover its running costs. Those women refuse as they say they are not benefiting from the solar panels. There is some discord here.'

What interests Salif is seeing whether or not solar-powered irrigation from a well is viable: whether sufficient land can be irrigated for it to be profitable. Of course, if all the equipment is provided for free, it is bound to be economically viable, as the running costs of solar power are almost negligible. But, for a scheme to work properly, it needs to make considerable profits, as the initial investments are high. It certainly does not look as if this is the case here. Working only about half a hectare of vegetables, utilizing no organic farming systems that increase yields and reduce input costs, and with obvious fundamental management and organizational problems, this project is simply helping a limited group of women make some profits in the short term. As soon as there are any serious problems, more than likely it will fold, as is so often the case with projects that are not sufficiently thought through and monitored. I have seen it often enough, as indeed when Salif and I made a research trip to the far south of Senegal in order to visit another solar-powered irrigation project, one that claimed to have set up a dozen such schemes.

This was my and Salif's most ambitious research foray to

date, but one we thought worth making. We travelled south by plane, flying first from Nouakchott to Dakar, capital of Senegal, then south over The Gambia to the southern Senegalese Casamance region.

It was a strange trip. In Casamance, we found ourselves in an entirely different Africa. This was the humid, colorful, tropical south. It could not have been more different from Mauritania. Gone was the formality and bearing of desert or near-desert people. Gone was the clean, stripped scarcity of life. Gone were the glare and the great heat, and gone was the horizon. Here instead were people who slopped around as though made from soft wax; here were scents and spicy smells around every corner; red earth and grass and endless trees. Even the traditional three glasses of tea so common across so much of West Africa were absent here, much to Salif's dismay. 'It's my drug,' he lamented.

The large, friendly director of the local development group in charge of the solar project we had come to see took us in his four-wheel drive on a tour of the forested countryside, becoming increasingly less communicative as it became clear that the projects did not exist: we found only one, which itself was not at that moment functioning.

'We've had problems,' he said. 'There have been funding issues.'

We do not linger long in the vegetable gardens of Danodine. It is excessively hot and the president of the co-operative looks as if she has work to get on with. We are also tempted away by the man who has attached himself to us, who invites us to his home for a rest and some refreshments.

Our new friend introduces himself as Issmou Kah: Salif vaguely knows him. He is tall and bright eyed with a mop of wild hair. He seems excessively pleased to see us. 'Danodine is a good place,' he enthuses as we walk to the Toyota. 'It is where my heart is. I was away for many years working as a teacher in the north, but I have come back. A man cannot deny his roots. He cannot forget his home.'

We rumble over the plain to Issmou's house: a single, sizeable mud-brick building with a tin roof and a veranda. We are installed in a room and provided with a jug of sweetened, powdered milk. Later a platter of rice and fish is produced by his wife, which we eat watched by his many small, wide-eyed children. Issmou is eloquent about the problems of Danodine. He has even produced a full printed and bound report on them, a copy of which he insists I take. The report, which I read then and there, is like a call to arms: an impassioned appeal to the residents of Danodine to reflect on their past, present and future; to mend their differences and strive to save their home from the annihilation he sees coming. For Issmou is very sure about the current state of affairs.

'This town is dying,' he says. 'All the young men are leaving. Only old men and women are left. No-one wants to live here. And why is this? Not just because of the droughts; it is because there is division amongst us. We are Africans,' he laughs, 'and so we argue. No-one can agree on anything. Everybody is arguing. Everybody is jealous of each other. But we can save this town. We can find solutions to our problems. It rests with us. We need only to come together, to drop our differences and work together.'

Issmou's oration is stirring, and I feel that Salif and I are the only audience he has had for some while. I ask him how he earns a living now that he no longer teaches.

'That is a problem,' he says. 'I have some fields, some sheep...' He does not finish.

When we leave, I ask Salif about what Issmou has said, confident that Salif, as always, will know the full story. Salif does not have much sympathy. 'Danodine,' he says wearily. 'has many problems.'

Prime among these, he tells me, is that when the tarmac road to Kaédi was built, some 15 years ago, it was put in the wrong place, bypassing the town.

'During the planning phase,' he says, 'the inhabitants were asked whether they wanted the road to pass directly through their town or not, but the town chief was against this and used his authority to overrule those of the opinion that the road would bring prosperity to the town. The chief was not in disagreement with this, but he argued that it would be much the same if it passed just nearby. What actually happened, though, was that when the road was built, instead of being put right next to the town, as the chief had wanted, it was put where it is now, four kilometers away. This was too far, meaning the town not only failed to profit from being on the road, but whatever trade had come through it on the old road dwindled. Many of the town's people,' Salif says, 'blame this on the chief and are angry with him. This is just one of the problems the town has,' he adds.

Another of them, and the most recent, Salif tells me, relates to a large tract of common land to the north of the town, which is said to have been leased to an American company that wishes to grow wheat there. The area in question extends to some 20,000 hectares, which is vast, and it seems incredible that anyone can be thinking of growing such a moisture-dependent crop in such a dry area when all the water will need to be pumped either from the ground or from a small river some kilometers distant. Nothing is for sure just yet, Salif tells me, and it might be only rumor, but it is said that members of two of the bigger families in Danodine have done a deal with the government agency that has granted the lease to the American company. They claim that traditional ownership of the land in question lies with them as they are the only families to have grown crops on any scale on the land for the last decade. The land, Salif says, is at a high elevation and so rarely used for crops, except by the pastoralists who grow only small patches of millet there, as well as pasturing their livestock.

'It is common land,' Salif says, 'and the town is divided on how to deal with the problem.'

Those who have pastoralist branches, he says, and use the area for grazing livestock are naturally against the sale of the land; those who are affiliated in any way to the two families who are involved in the deal are of the opinion that some benefit will accrue to them. If the land purchase, or land grab, as such opaque deals are increasingly being termed, does take place, in all likelihood all that will happen is that, for the period of the contract, the land will be depleted of nutrients, the rivers and ground sources of water, and the traditional farmers of labor. Then it will fold due to lack of new investment or mismanagement or just general non-viability and everyone will be much worse off than before.

Meagre resources lead to competition, confrontations and power struggles. When I look out of the Toyota window as we pull away from Danodine, I wonder just how anyone manages to survive in such a desiccated and apparently desolate land. By this time of year – the end of the dry, cooler season – there is barely a blade of dried grass left. But there are whole communities down here and survive they do, if only just. This has always been marginal country where there is only a thin line between survival and non-survival. People have evolved coping mechanisms to deal with it. The only trouble is, that line is becoming increasingly thinner as climate change takes an ever stronger grip and drought, flood and mismanagement take their toll.

We arrive at Kaédi, the main regional town of the south, in the late afternoon. Kaédi is an unusual place. By any normal standards it does not have much to recommend it. It is, as one particular traveller's blog I read bluntly put it, 'a shithole in the arse of the world: there is no reason to go there'.

Dating mainly from the colonial era and built originally along traditional French colonial lines, Kaédi might just have been acceptable then, although I suspect anyone posted here would not have been on the fast track to promotion: a couple of wide, tree-lined avenues with a few colonial bungalows set back in spacious compounds; a small, central commercial district and enclosed marketplace; administrative buildings; the post office and European club; outlying districts of mud-brick 'native' dwellings. It sat then, as now, in the grip of a rocky plain of black, shattered hills in one of the hottest places on the globe. Today it is in ruins. Decades of the marginalization of the South have led to such neglect that in places the town seems to have disintegrated. Travelling around it is like being in a disaster zone: smashed buildings, destroyed roads, rotting piles of rubbish with dead livestock thrown in: a dejected, windblown-looking populace.

For such a very dry region, it is surprising how much of this damage is due to rain. Homes built of mud bricks are half washed away, the inhabitants living in the remains. Unpaved roads are so riven by run-off channels that they are no longer passable. Whole districts are cleaved by newly carved dry riverbeds. The complete lack of upkeep or investment in the town has resulted in its becoming a degraded backwater that looks like a rubbish tip. There is no public transport for its hundred thousand inhabitants, nor, until very recently, any taxis either. Electricity supply and telecommunications are sporadic. There are only four doctors in the town, and barely a hotel, restaurant or public space; there are no cinemas and few streetlights: in fact Kaédi lacks just about anything one would normally associate with an urban center. And all the trees have been cut down.

On the other hand, the town, because of its neglect, has not suffered the burgeoning population growth that is typical in West Africa. In a way it is still a very traditional place: a rural focal point more than an urban center. Although its outlying districts appear mostly depopulated, the center is one big marketplace, where nomads leading camels brush shoulders with peasants leading sheep, women carrying baskets of vegetables and the inevitable overladen donkey-carts. Military Landcruisers, in from the desert, shoulder through, a posse of fierce-looking turbaned soldiers clasping rifles in the back. The massive articulated trucks on their way south or north somehow negotiate the close-packed streets. Hardware merchandise spills out of the lines of merchants' boutiques: pick handles, fencing wire, drums of cooking oil, a hundredweight of soap cakes, 10 tons of cement. There is something about the roughened, frontier-like atmosphere of the place that I rather like.

Salif and I have been discussing what to do about our transport problem. We will look for another starter-motor, which Amadou Tall still insists is the problem. I have my doubts, but then I am no mechanic. We drive to the garage, which is the central area of town where transport vehicles congregate. Here the wrecks of abandoned vehicles mingle with the wrecks of still-functioning ones, great trucks gun their engines amid vast plumes of black smoke, men swagger about shouting, ragged beggars beg and touts seek custom for their long-range charges.

We head across the garage to an area behind a row of eating shacks where there is a mechanic's workshop. By now the sun is low and much tinkering takes place under the engine cover. An hour passes and we set off. It is 32 kilometers now to

Keniéba. The vehicle is running, just. We fill it with diesel and make our way to the police post at the exit to town. Unlike the many roadblocks we have passed up to now, perhaps 20 in all, including a couple of the new, feared 'no negotiation' squads, here the police are not interested in our IDs. They are friendly in a condescending way and wave us through. We are now off the tarmac, away from the connection that it gives to the other, more modern and official world and the presence of a foreigner is enough to give us free passage.

At sundown, we stop for prayers. My companions form a line and bow their heads to Allah. I sit on an anthill and smoke a cigarette. Then we are on again, into the night, part of the time following the piste, or built dirt road, part of the time veering off on the myriad tracks that weave, like snakes, through the bush. Then we are there, in Keniéba, Salif's village, an arrival I have experienced so many times, and one that has barely changed in all the years I have been coming: the rushed crowd of children each eager to shake my and Salif's hands; the smiling faces of the adults looming out of the dark; the procession down the thin, sandy ways to Salif's family's compound. Mats are quickly spread out for us as we are surrounded by the uproar of a hundred excited children and the metronomically repeated words of traditional greeting. Later, we are brought a platter of roasted chicken, and tea is made. Later still I am shown to 'my' room, where a mosquito net has been hung over a foam mattress on the floor. Here, as always, I sleep like a log.

4 Keniéba

Rhythms of the morning… Mariam's spirit… The art of rural toiletry… An interview with the Adjutant… The exorbitant cost of free housing… Living with water in a parched land… The irrigation scheme

Morning: I lie under my mosquito net listening to the familiar sounds of early morning life. I have been awake since before dawn. This is mainly due to the cockerels. Keniéba is known as a village because in most respects its life functions like a village. In reality, though, it is a small town of several thousand inhabitants. How many families this breaks down into, I do not know, but each and every family compound, containing perhaps 60 or 70 people, contains at least a couple of cockerels. Across the whole town, this adds up to a lot.

First one crows, then, tentatively, another follows suit. A moment of silence, then a couple more give it a go. Then gradually they all wake up and begin clearing their throats. Before long the cacophony of voices – some tiny and far, some loud and close – fills the air. It is still dark, but soon the thinnest of lights is seeping into the air. In the compounds, shrouded figures are emerging from mosquito nets and rooms, still mute for the moment in the privacy of the pre-dawn world.

I know the routine. I have watched it often enough. Soon the women, their shawls pulled over their heads, will be working with bent backs and small hand-held brushes at the patches of sand outside their rooms, sweeping them in little clouds of dust of the previous day's debris. Menfolk, off to the fields, will have taken a quick breakfast in their rooms and will be loading a donkey with provisions or slipping quietly away with a hoe across their backs. A woman will free a milking cow from the livestock enclosure and milk it into a calabash. Then the kids and lambs will be released and dive excitedly for their mothers' teats, butting them to loosen the milk. It is still early and, in the huts, schoolchildren will be hunched over bowls of yesterday's leftovers or, if they are lucky, sticks of coarse bread dipped in mugs of chicory. Then they are off, as are the livestock, which weave their way like commuters to the plains outside town where a herder will gather them up to take them out for the day's browsing.

It is now that the women's work begins in earnest: to-ing and fro-ing like ants to the nearest well, great basins of water balanced on their heads; tending the infants; washing clothes; preparing food for the day – an endless litany of heavy chores. Later they may have to walk many kilometers to collect firewood, or perhaps they will have duties in the fields such as bird scaring or winnowing. The rhythmic thud as they mill grain in the compounds, throwing their long wooden pestles high in the air before bringing them down into the wooden mortars, reverberates like a heartbeat throughout the town.

Since before dawn Amadou Tall has been driving the *piste* back to Kaédi where Salif has sent him to see if he can effect any permanent repairs to the Toyota. We are without a vehicle now.

I emerge from my room to find Salif's wife, Mariam, busying herself about the earthen corridor of the house. She greets me and asks after my wife and children. She is shy and formal, but only briefly. Mariam is a lively, bright, indomitable spirit. She was born and brought up in a city, and most of her married life has been spent in a town. According to her, village life is 'very bad', but this is always said with such provocative good humor, one knows she is not complaining. For Mariam is not the complaining type. She has borne Salif eight children, two of whom died in infancy, and the strain visible on her otherwise bright face tells of the effort she makes in all she does. She is passionate and verbal and no doubt ruffled a few feathers when she first set up home in Salif's family compound. But it is always she, I notice, who raises spirits when people are tired and despondent; it is she who thwacks the children if they are misbehaving, who fusses most when they are ill, who pulls the old folk's legs to get them laughing. But she does not cope well with the heat and is often ill at the hottest times of year. She also has a morbid fear of the rainy season, convinced, she tells me, that the roof of their house is going to fall on her head. She is the antithesis to Salif's cool: lively, passionate and unpredictable.

She shouts out of the doorway to the compound for someone to fetch me the *bidon*, the plastic kettle-shaped container from which people wash hands. She then turns back to me and rattles off a line of Peul, bursting into laughter at my look of incomprehension. 'You don't understand?' she says in her poor French, knowing full well that my Peul is pathetic. She likes to tease me.

The *bidon* is produced and I go out back to wash.

Salif's family compound consists of eight or so oblong buildings enclosing a large yard, one end of which is taken up with livestock pens. Each building houses a different subfamily and is constructed in the traditional manner out of sun-baked mud bricks with a smooth mud and cow-dung finish. The constructions are brown and earthy, the three or four dark rooms inside limited to the breadth of the gnarled tree branches from which the ceiling rafters are made and over which a mud and cow-dung mix is plastered to form the roof. The buildings are considerably cooler than their modern equivalents with tin roofs and concrete block walls but they suffer from rain erosion and need to be rebuilt every 10 or 15 years. Out back of each is the small, open space where ablutions are performed, to where I now head.

There is much that can be written about the peculiarities of the village toiletry experience. I will be brief, mentioning only that this unavoidable necessity is not for the fainthearted and that the 'long-drop' method is fine in principle but in reality has its limitations due to the complete lack of any emptying system and the large number of flies and other insects that like to make their home there. At night, it is a tricky act balancing above the noisome pile while spotlighting the commando raids of cockroaches around your feet. Perhaps it was better in the early days, before Salif's family had dug any of the many, now filled, latrines that surround their living quarters. Then, you simply walked out of town to the surrounding plain to do your thing. The trouble here was, first, that, when required, it was difficult to make a dash, and, second, my 'movements' tended to become a matter of public concern and my trips to the bush were often accompanied by a posse of well-wishers, whose anticipation did nothing for my regularity. And you had to watch very carefully where you trod.

The compound is bright and hot by the time I make my way into it. Salif and a group of men are seated on a raised earthen dais in the shade of a building on the far side. I make my way towards them, shaking hands around the compound as I go. These are people I have known for many years. It is a strange relationship I have had with them, turning up once a year for a couple of weeks. To me, it is like a freeze-frame: the compound and family always look much the same – some people gone, some new faces, a newly rendered building, a new toilet perhaps – but essentially little has changed. Looking back over time, of course, I can see other changes: infants growing into youths, rice replacing couscous as the staple diet, mobile phones becoming common. But those things that really matter have altered very little: the same respect for age is paramount; a devout adherence to a moderate and tolerant interpretation of Islam is universal; deference to the family – putting its needs over those of the individual – is total; and the overriding dilapidation of a poverty born of a disintegrating climate and dysfunctional regime remains the same. For Salif's family, though, my visits must seem quite different. The time between each one constitutes just short of a full year. My appearance amongst them must be like that of a perennial: something noticed but soon forgotten in the whirl of everyday existence; not, as for me, a landmark in the year around which much else is shaped.

I greet Abou, Salif's younger brother, an odd young man with a ready smile but a reluctance to communicate beyond this. In all the years I have known him, we have probably not spoken more than a dozen words at a time. He is married to Uma, a young woman with hands like a blacksmith's and eyes full of mirth. She seems to have had a baby strapped to her back for more years than I can remember and I cannot ever remember seeing her when she was not working.

Mamadou, a first cousin of Salif's, ducks under the low thatch of his veranda to shake my hand. 'Peter…' he exclaims, that familiar, half-shy, half-defensive expression on his face. Mamadou has a reputation – fair or unfair I do not know – for being work shy, although I have seen him often enough in the fields and also working as a carpenter. He is a friendly, if abrasive, character but always makes a point of lending me his radio whenever I am visiting, thoughtfully tuned already to the BBC World Service.

I stoop under the thatch to shake hands with his old mother where she sits on the floor next to their doorway. This remarkable old lady can no longer use her legs and seems content to sit here from morning to night. Indeed, she has sat there for so many years that I cannot remember a time when she did not. In the mornings, when the sun's rays are low, a screen of sackcloth is erected to shade her. Throughout the day, she shells groundnuts, chops vegetables and picks stones from platters of rice. She chats with elderly companions who drop by. Mostly, though, she just sits thumbing her prayer beads, smiling silently to herself.

Harouna, a tall, well-built young man, back for the moment from his *aventures* in Congo Brazzaville, where he works, greets me shyly. He has just got married and is in the middle of constructing a small house for himself, squeezing it in between two others like a shiny new denture in a row of rotten ones. Ismail, a lanky, hard-working farmer with hands like pieces of wood, is more confident in his welcome. He shares a house with his widowed father, who surprised everyone last year by marrying a woman 40 years his junior and promptly siring a baby. The old man always makes a point of coming solemnly up to me on my first night back and delivering a long, official welcome. The last time he did this, Mariam embarrassed him by pointing to his wife and baby nearby, remarking: 'He is old, but look what he has done,' at which the old man's face broke into a wide, sheepish grin.

Many others come up to shake my hand once I have seated myself next to Salif on the dais, some faces I hardly know, some people whose names I should know but don't. There are probably as many as 70 direct family members living in Salif's family's compound at any one time, with a roving population of perhaps the same again. The wider family, of course, is far larger, extending from the closer relations in different compounds in Keniéba itself, to those who reside permanently in the capital or elsewhere. The still-larger circle of the family takes in a vast amount of people dotted throughout this part of Africa, from ancient branches in villages and towns in Mali, to more recent ones in Senegal and throughout southern Mauritania. The largest circle of course encompasses virtually anyone of the same ethnic group with whom, more often than not, some family connection can be found. The extremity of this network goes even beyond this, manifesting itself most clearly amongst newly arrived expatriate Africans in the cities of the world where the simple fact of being black and African is enough to be classed as a 'brother' from whom help can be requested.

For my breakfast, Mariam produces a pot of boiling water with some bananas and dried biscuits – good bland food, for she knows I often have 'difficulties' with my stomach when I visit the village. 'Salif?' she says, holding out her hand.

Salif knows what she is after and digs into his famously bottomless *bobo* chest pocket, producing first a wheel bearing, then a packet of seeds, then two half-cannibalized mobile phones, many scraps of paper with numbers written on them, some letters, three wads of cash and, finally, after a struggle in the deepest recesses, a Lipton's teabag. Mariam sits on the edge of the dais by my feet, dipping the teabag into a glass of the boiling water. A large man approaches.

'Rock,' Salif greets him. Rock is a relation from the compound next door, a giant of a man whom I have known many years and the only person in Keniéba ever to ask me for anything. For years he was after my watch, then some money. He is an educated man and spent many years away from the village and is now bogged down with too many dependants, no money and, according to Salif, a reluctance to work.

'Rock,' Mariam echoes Salif, though with a combative glint in her eye.

Rock grins broadly and greets me. 'You have not been to

visit me!' he exclaims with mock hurt as he shakes my hand.

'How could he come to visit you, you old fool?' Mariam bursts in. 'He only arrived last night.' She laughs, getting up off the dais, and Rock pushes her playfully. Mariam staggers off across the compound laughing loudly. 'Take a seat, Rock,' she says as she goes.

Rock is a little embarrassed by all this, but not unduly so, and sits down to chat with me, telling me how hard life is as a peasant. 'Work, work, work. Toil, toil, toil. That's all it is. We plant crops for the birds and locusts to eat. Ah, but we are strong... we endure,' he says with a strong hint of irony.

I am aware that there is tension between Salif's and Rock's families but I have never got much out of Salif about it.

'You will come to visit me before you go,' Rock demands when he gets up to leave. I tell him, as usual, that I will try to, knowing I probably will not.

Mid-morning, by which time most of the shade in which we are sitting on the dais has been swallowed up. Salif and I decide to relocate ourselves across town to the *Centre*, the building from which our activities take place that Salif's development group constructed some years previously. We have much paperwork to do.

Keniéba is roughly divided into two separate sections: the traditional town inhabited by Black Africans, and the more modern part centered on the main east-west road. The former is a warren of sandy passageways winding behind the half-dissolved walls of the large, interlocking family compounds and ending up in a small commercial center with its covered market and *boutiques*, as the small, basic shops that line every street in Mauritania are known. Moors and their many dozens of trading *boutiques* dominate the newer part of town up by the road, which, alive with commerce and activity, day-by-day eclipses its older, more traditional neighbor.

We make our way through the old town, down the winding

passageways and through the near-deserted commercial area. Here a phalanx of old men, with whom we perform the prolonged ritualistic greetings of hand shaking and enquiries after health and family, sit under a central tree.

The old part of town is placed on the edge of a natural flood plain of baked earth, to the south of which scrub and brush run to the Moshe, a tributary of the Senegal River. To the north, the land rises gently to the road, beyond which is an infinity of gravelly plain. We pass up to the road with its traders' *boutiques*, trucks and roadside restaurants. Beyond is the newest part of the new town, where the transformation of rural existence to urban, of Peul culture to Moor, of the traditional to the modern, takes place before your eyes. At the back, where the plains roll in, giving way to inclines of sand, the newly arrived nomadic Moors, inexorably driven south by the drying of the desert, set up their camps. Only a few hundred meters further in, and there are small, cement box-houses attached to their tents. A little further in, and the boxes are enlarged and have small boutiques included. Further in still, and the houses are larger and there is no sign of tent left at all.

It is here that the *Gendarmerie* is to be found, where the Adjutant, the local military chief, resides. Salif thinks it diplomatic to pay our respects. What with the upcoming elections, and the existent threat al-Qaeda and its affiliates pose in many parts of West Africa, a certain tension prevails that it would be best not to ignore. The recent uprisings in the neighboring country of Mali, partially Islamist in nature, have inspired increased activity among the security forces in Mauritania and there have been instances of terrorism in the country, notably the kidnapping and killing of some foreigners – admittedly some time ago now.

The *Gendarmerie* is a dark, block building of three near-empty rooms, in one of which we find the Adjutant sitting on the floor making tea. He is a well-turned out young man in a starched military uniform: confident and casual, with watchful eyes. He greets us politely and listens to Salif's representations. He nods; gives me an appraising look.

'You have been here before?' he asks.

'Many times,' I reply.

'It is good,' he says. *'Bismillah'* – welcome, in the name of Allah. He turns back to his tea making and Salif and I leave. As we make our way towards the *Centre*, which is nearby, I remark that the Adjutant seems 'okay'. Salif is not in agreement.

'I do not have confidence in that man,' he says darkly.

'What do you mean?' I ask.

'I do not trust him.'

This surprises me. 'Why not?' The man did not seem to me any different from the many military types we come across daily in Mauritania.

Salif's answer is enigmatic: 'Between bandits and those charged with protecting you from them,' he says, 'there is often a relationship.' And, as if to confirm these disturbing thoughts, at that moment Salif's mobile rings. It is the Adjutant.

'He says we are to let him know exactly when and where we are going each time we go into the countryside,' Salif says, even darker now, when he has finished the short conversation.

We discuss the matter further. I feel quite sure Salif is being unnecessarily paranoid. Certainly, in Mauritania the security forces have always used any supposed security threat as an excuse to increase their control of the population as a whole – and, indeed, any enhanced al-Qaeda threat certainly strengthens the regime's hand for more 'support' from the international community – but whether members of the security forces are actually in cahoots with the terrorists, or bandits, as Salif calls them, I do not know. And the few Islamist problems there are in the country are far to the east. There have been no reported issues in this region at all. It is unusual for Salif to be unsettled in this manner. But then the rumor machine in Africa, I know from experience, is deeply pervasive. And Salif no doubt feels a strong sense of responsibility for me. He wants to play it safe and I am happy with that. We agree that we will call the Adjutant but only at the moment we are leaving town, as in this way he will not have time to contact any dodgy associates who might wish to come and waylay me. I try to keep my face straight as we walk, not wishing to undermine the seriousness Salif is attaching to the matter. I suspect the whole melodrama is more to do with the fact that he has taken a dislike to the Adjutant. Both his manner and his role are anathema to Salif.

Shortly, we come to the *Centre*, which is a large, concrete building in a compound surrounded on all sides by a wall. Here we settle down with our papers on the floor of the spacious main room and begin going through the accounts, sweating our way through the figures as Abou, Salif's younger brother, who has appeared, supplies us with a succession of teas. By the time we move on to project reports, it is already afternoon. Still we keep at it, eventually synthesizing all to a number of primary issues: the problems of our nascent well-digging program and the, to me, incomprehensible failure of the community for whom we are digging the well to provide draught donkeys, the only input required of them; the apparent 'drift' of our successful Dohley Women's market garden project from its original aims; and my concern over the tractor-ploughing service Salif and his group provide, which might, I feel, be leading farmers into an unsustainable dependence on a mode of machinery-based agriculture they cannot afford.

Finally, there is the matter of the Toyota. If it fails to materialize, as seems likely, how the hell are we going to manage the two-day seminar that has been arranged for this week? Many months of organization have gone into this meeting, during which the delegates from many ethnic groupings will come together to agree on objectives for the large community project Salif is in the process of developing. Neither of us has met Ibrahim Tandia, the Senegalese development consultant we will be picking up in Kaédi tomorrow who will be leading the seminar, but much rests on him. Mobility will be essential, not just to get him here, but also to bring in many of the seminar delegates who live in remote areas.

The afternoon is well advanced by the time we finish and the heat is shattering, as though the hot season, which is imminent, has already arrived. Temperatures of 40 or even 45 degrees are not uncommon in the hot season, which lasts from April to July, at which time the rains can start.

'Mariam will have food for us,' Salif says encouragingly, noticing the depleted state I am in. We pack up our papers and, indeed, when we arrive back in the family compound, three large platters of food await us, around which we quickly settle down with a crowd of many others. Salif ladles the stew of steaming vegetables and fish onto the platters of rice, and we eat. The small river nearby, the Moshe, kept full throughout the year by dams at either end, produces a remarkable quantity of fish for the population of Keniéba. There are various types, but the best is a member of the large catfish family, whose fleshy meat is deliciously nutty. This, along with freshly cut okra, sweet potato, yam and carrots in a rich tomato and onion sauce, produces a delicious meal, spiced with chili.

There must be 30 or more people hunched around the meal. Salif tells me the family gets through over two 25-kilo sacks of rice per week, plus quantities of millet couscous, vegetables, fish and bread. In theory, the couscous comes from the millet crop the family plants during the rainy season, and the rice comes from the irrigation scheme Salif set up all those years ago, as do the vegetables. In practice, no year works quite like this and differing amounts of these always need to be bought in, along with the quantities of tomato paste, salt and cooking oil used in the cuisine. Sheep and goats are slaughtered only for special occasions. Following the universal law that decrees capacity is always matched by need, even the very best of years never produces enough for all the hungry mouths.

We settle down under a thatch for the rest of the afternoon. By early evening I am up and keen to start out for Mabafé, the family irrigation scheme that we have planned to visit today, eight kilometers to the south. Salif's enthusiasm for the expedition, however, does not match my burning need, despite the heat, to do something active. He turns to Harouna, the young man back from Congo Brazzaville who is preparing the last of the afternoon's three glasses of tea, and asks if he would like to accompany me.

'Of course,' the young man replies without hesitation.

And so it is agreed: Salif will stay back and Harouna will accompany me. We will not call the Adjutant as I will not be going far. Amadou Tall, Salif tells me before we leave, has called. He has left the Toyota with a mechanic who says there is a problem with the radiator. The vehicle will not be serviceable for tomorrow. We shall instead have to take a bush taxi to Kaédi in the morning and look for a vehicle to hire.

We set off for Mabafé out of the rear of the compound. This backs directly onto the flood plain at the edge of town. Nearby is an extensive area of pits where young men labor, digging out the clayey soil that they pack into brick moulds and then lay out in patterns on the ground to bake in the sun. The bricks, Harouna tells me as we make our way around the pits, although cheap individually, end up costing a lot, as even a small house like the one he is building in the compound will consume nearly 6,000 of them. I ask him how much his house will cost to build, and he tells me he will have to outlay the equivalent of $3,000. This is a figure I find astonishing and I

ask him why it will cost this much. Surely, I say, most of the materials are virtually free.

'Nothing is free here,' he says brusquely. I press him further. Surely he and his family can at least provide most of the labor for free.

'Mostly, yes,' he says, 'but I will have to pay for all their food. And there's also the wood for the rafters to be paid for and all the loads of earth and cow dung for the render and mortar, which have to be brought in by donkey-cart, as does all the water to mix with them. There's much to be paid for.' The reality, of course, is that life here, as elsewhere, is not cheap.

We walk on in silence. I must have known Harouna since he was a child, although the truth is I do not remember him. He seems a little ill at ease. I have come across this before from expatriates, those who live away from their villages in the cities of the world. It is not always easy for them when they return to their homes, and it is not made any easier when they find me there. They are unsure of how to react to me, and fear being patronized. I ask him how long he intends on staying now that he is back home.

'A couple of years,' he says.

'It is hard coming back?' I say.

He laughs. 'You have no idea. Working in the fields! It is very difficult when you are no longer used to it. There's nothing to do in the evenings. And you have to be a good man. When you come back to the village you put on your *bobo*, you throw away your cigarettes and you pray five times a day.'

We make our way across the floodplain away from Keniéba and enter an area of scrubby bush through which the sandy track weaves. Small doves flutter off at our approach, and high above, a harrier circles on a thermal.

In the early days of my visits to Keniéba, the countryside around the town looked all much the same to me. Parts of it were sandy, parts hard, baked earth, parts dotted with scrub and stunted trees. But it was all dry and of much the same level. It was only as time went on that I began to understand that this was not the case. Indeed, it was fairly flat country, but not entirely so, and it was these small variations in height, I discovered, sometimes as little as a meter, that made all the difference. This is because of the nature of the rainfall. Coming, as it does, in large downpours after a long dry season when the ground has been baked to a concrete hardness, runoff is extremely rapid, quickly filling the dry riverbeds, or *oueds*, that drain into larger rivers, which in turn flow into the Senegal River. The speed with which this all takes place means flooding is inevitable and indeed, in a normal year, vast areas can be inundated. This is not a problem as the inhabitants of the region have situated their villages in places that are above all but the most exceptional floods and have shaped their agricultural practices around this event.

It is the speed with which the water drains from the land that is so significant. Only tiny variations in elevation can mean the difference between land that drains in an hour, land that holds water for a week, and land that dries up over the period of three months. These, in conjunction with soil types, dictate exactly to what use each part of the land can be put. The higher sandy areas, for example, which drain the fastest, are good only for brief pastures. Land with a higher clay content, say in a slight depression, will hold water for a little longer, allowing sufficient water penetration for a quick crop of sorghum to be grown. Land lower still, where the water takes even longer to drain away, can be planted with millet. And the land with the highest clay content at the lowest elevation, even though perhaps still only a few meters below the highest ground, constitutes the primary agricultural area where millet and maize can be grown in abundance in a good year.

The exact annual precipitation and precise level of the preceding floods are therefore vital. A minor reduction in the rainfall and decrease in the floods can leave huge areas that normally produce crops high and dry. Then again, years that have exceptional rainfall can cause havoc, flooding villages, washing away crops and stranding livestock. If one throws in the fact that the densities of livestock in the south have risen hugely in recent years, due to a general migration from the dryer north – livestock that can cause untold damage to unfenced crops – it becomes clear how very marginal and

vulnerable life is in the region.

Traditionally, the manner in which people survive is to have a mixture of economic practices. Any one family, for example, might have a pastoral branch, where livestock herders are prepared, when necessary, to range far and wide in search of pastures. The families might also have access to tracts of the higher crop-growing land. And the majority of them will probably also have traditional entitlement to parts of the more fertile low-lying areas. In addition, certain family members might be involved in trade or artisanal occupations. This all lends them a flexibility that enables them to deal with the vagaries of what has always been a volatile climate. At least that is how it worked until the parameters of that volatility started to stretch and climate change began to take its toll. Now things are not so simple.

One response people have had to climate change has been to set up irrigation schemes, as Salif's family have done. This, they reason, represents a way forward. Intensive cash crops can be grown using mechanized farming methods that will drag production systems out of the subsistence level at the same time as mitigating the effects of drought. This is the theory upon which the hydrology of the region was altered back in the 1980s, thanks to a vast project that saw large dams built on the Senegal River and its tributaries. Inevitably, this was a controversial project. On the one hand, it did seem a logical response to the devastating droughts of the preceding decade, allowing for a vastly increased amount of irrigated agriculture in the Senegal River Valley, as well as producing hydroelectric power. On the other hand, amongst a score of other controversial issues, the traditional annual flooding of the river valley, upon which large numbers of people depended for their livelihoods, would be affected. The floods, in the receding waters of which people planted their crops, would now occur only in the very wettest of years. Years of poor rain would result in no floods at all.

A small-scale irrigation sector centered on the region around Keniéba has grown up. At best, though, this is a sector that is struggling to survive; at worst, it is simply a means by which a lot of people lose a lot of money. This is because it functions so inefficiently in such unfavorable conditions. The costs of inputs, from pumps, through the fuel for them, to fertilizers and pesticides, continually rise. Rice is inefficiently mono-cropped. Water from huge pumps is flooded in the most wasteful manner onto huge fields of onions, which then fetch low prices at market because a thousand tons of subsidized Dutch ones have just descended upon the markets in Nouakchott. Banks give loans at extortionate rates, often requiring farmers to take machinery of poor quality instead of cash. There are the numerous natural problems to deal with: locusts, bird invasions, floods. And then a pump will break down at just the wrong moment. Or a bag of seed purchased will be of such poor quality that it does not germinate. Or weed management will be sub-standard. Or a cartel of Moorish merchants will have doubled the price of fertilizer. The list of what can and does go wrong is endless and what is remarkable is not that so many of the schemes fold after only a few years, but that many struggle on for so long. One such is Salif's family scheme, Mabafé.

The last of the sun's rays are disappearing as we approach the wire-mesh fence that surrounds Mabafé. Here lie 20 hectares of arable land divided into *planches*, plots of land some 200 meters square. Some 32 families grow crops on these *planches*, paying half their harvest to Salif's family in return for the land, the tractor work used in preparing it each season and the water that irrigates it. Two large pumps are stationed by the Moshe River, which runs adjacent to the scheme, and which, by the use of dams at either end, has a year-round supply of water. This water, once drawn from the river by the pumps, is run onto the land through a network of mud channels and sluices. The main crop is rice, grown during the rainy season, from June to October. Some families will then plant vegetables or some maize, but not many do this.

The creation and development of the scheme has been an ongoing story for many years. It is the result of years of labor and perseverance, often in the face of the most overwhelming difficulties. Years of exceptional rains have led to the inundation of entire crops, meaning the loss of the entire year's harvest and profit. There have been problems with pumps breaking down at key moments and with bird and locust invasions. There always seems to be a problem. And, as with farmers the world over, the costs of the next year's inputs are covered through loans and, when there is no harvest, or a poor harvest, these loans cannot be repaid. But the families persevere, and somehow Salif's family, which owns the scheme, has managed over the years to stay afloat, even investing when they can in new machinery and land. The fence ringing the scheme is the newest of these investments.

It is the quiet season now, the rice having been harvested back in October and the main vegetable crop also being at an end. Many of the *planches*, I see as we arrive, have been ploughed up, on some of which livestock are browsing crop residues. There are only a few people about – those who are growing hot-season vegetables and teams of youths improving water channels in preparation for the following rice crop.

The guardian, a tall, thin man who lives with his wife and children in a camp on the edge of the scheme, greets us. He, Harouna and some others then line up for the sundown prayers. Touching their hands to the earth, they symbolically wash themselves, then stand for the introductory prayers before bowing in homage to Allah three times, pressing their foreheads to the earth. As they rise up, each of them has a small disc of sand imprinted on his head, like a talisman. There is a donkey cart heading back to Keniéba on which we can cadge a lift.

We are a cheerful bunch as we trot along in the evening light: Harouna and I; women with baskets; men with hoes. Each time we come to a place where the ground is rutted, the cart comes almost to a standstill, creaking slowly over the iron-hard earth. Then the driver jigs the donkey up again, and, with a few taps of his stick and a whoop, we are off, the rapidly darkening bush slipping quietly by to the clop of the donkey's hooves. Before we are back it is dark, our surroundings illuminated only by the canopy of stars and that strange luminosity the plains seem to emit at night, as though they were releasing a tiny fraction of the sunlight that has poured on them all day.

Back in the compound, the full swing of the evening has passed. Livestock are shut up. Social groups have split. Salif is waiting for me on the mats and cushions Mariam puts out each evening in front of their house. 'How was Mabafé?' he asks.

'It was good,' I reply. 'But there is not much happening there just now.'

'It's true,' he says, 'but you had a good walk.'

5 To Kaédi

Learning good humor... The old merchant... Salif's sons... The local agronomist... A hometown's lost heyday... Our consultant arrives... Death and Allah's fields... Alisanne's adventures in Europe... The infinite heavens

Salif calls into my room shortly after dawn. One of the elusive bush taxis to Kaédi is about to depart, and he has arranged for it to pass the compound and pick us up. This is the result of an excellent piece of intelligence-gathering on Salif's behalf and is a bit of rare good fortune: transport between Keniéba and Kaédi can be difficult, and you can wait whole days for a bush taxi without success. Despite hastily preparing ourselves for departure, however, the minibus does not turn up for an hour and a half and then, having taken us no more than a kilometer around the edge of town, comes to a stop, steam hissing from under the engine cover.

Salif does not waste any time. Seeing a plume of dust rising on a nearby track, he rushes off to wave another vehicle down. A few minutes later he reappears with a van. We are in luck. It is bound for Kaédi and is departing immediately. Not so fortunately, although it is a large van of the usual bush-taxi variety, it has not been 'converted'. This usually means having holes cut into the sides for windows and a few benches bolted in the back. We will have none of these luxuries but instead must sit in the coffin-like interior on top of a consignment of rice sacks.

Fortunately, there are only a few other passengers. Unfortunately, the driver does not intend to let it remain this way. Only half an hour later, the back is filling up. Every village or camp we pass seems to have two or three people outside waiting for a lift. The driver cannot resist and, by the end, we are crammed to such an extent, our heads pressed against the ceiling, and it is so very hot and airless, that I am angry. I want to get out and remonstrate. This is absurd. It is dangerous. It is horrible. I cannot even imagine what the temperature must be in the back. But I do not. Like all the others, I let a stupor of discomfort and acceptance overcome me. It is a moment, I realize, for gritting teeth and getting through. Like all the others, I do not really have a choice. There may not be any other means of getting to Kaédi today. It comes as a tremendous relief when we get stuck in each of the sandy *oueds*, or dry riverbeds, we meet.

We stagger out the back, a colorful crowd standing incongruously on the pale sand of the *oued*. My anger has evaporated. In the face of the good humor of my fellow passengers, who seem able even now to find things to laugh about, I cannot maintain my *hauteur*. At one of the *oueds* we even have to unload the van's entire consignment of rice sacks in order to lighten the vehicle sufficiently to push it out. How can you take this seriously? How the passengers laugh when they are sprayed with sand from the spinning wheels. How thoughtful they are of each other when we arrange ourselves in the back once more, minimizing their own space in favor of their neighbors. Only one young woman is unhappy, crying for a while before resting her head on the shoulder of her friend or sister, who strokes her forehead as a mother does for a child. I do not know why she is crying, but I do not imagine it is anything to do with our discomfort.

Once in Kaédi we make for the house of Mamadou Kane, a

relation of Salif's whose home we are in the habit of using as a base when in town. It is here that Salif lodged when he was a student attending the Lycée and it is here that two of his sons, also at the Lycée, now lodge.

Mamadou Kane is an old man and one of the biggest merchants in town. Not for him, though, the trappings of wealth. This is a man and a merchant in the traditional mould. His house, dating from colonial times, though large and solidly built, is almost entirely devoid of material possessions. One dilapidated, empty, high-ceilinged room leads to the next, most of life focused on the wide, tiled veranda and central courtyard where chickens peck, pots and pans are scattered and miscellaneous dependants appear and disappear.

Mamadou Kane himself passes his time on a small mat in a distant corner of the veranda. He is tall and bent, with a kindly face and a pair of bottle-top glasses held together with masking tape. Equally ancient friends and business associates pass time with him on mats in his corner, and many hours are devoted to his prayer beads. You do not get the feeling, however, that his business is suffering as a result. The twinkle in the old man's eye speaks of a wily astuteness. His two sons may be off in America, apparently with little intention of returning, but he has obviously built his business with such a sound base that it is secure even in the near-dysfunctional environment of the south. At home, though, it is his wife who rules: a charming and welcoming lady whose casualness belies the strict atmosphere of compassion evident in her home. Mamadou Kane himself has for 15 years grinned at me without the slightest idea what to say next.

'And when are you going to do business with me?' he always asks finally, chuckling at his rhetorical question.

Over the years, I have spent many a night in Mamadou Kane's house. Generally, Salif and I sleep up on the flat roof of one of the buildings, for Kaédi, situated on its rocky plain between low shattered hills, is one of the very hottest places in the region, and hence the world. It also has a fearful mosquito problem and many a sleepless night have I spent there, as Mamadou Kane's house knows no mosquito nets. One night in particular, I was violently ill from something I had eaten. I remember a girl – a house servant – nursing me through the two subsequent, semi-delirious days: a girl with bright eyes, the darkest of black complexions and a voice as soft as down.

Salif's two sons are waiting for us at the door to Mamadou Kane's house. Mohammed and Saidou are two years apart in age, Mohammed 17 and Saidou 15. Saidou, like Salif, is bright and, despite the fact that he is younger than his brother, is in the same year as him at the Lycée. 'He is intelligent,' Salif says of Saidou. 'He passes all his exams with ease. Mohammed,' he says, 'does not like to work.'

Salif's relationship with his sons is, to the outsider, formal in the extreme. He greets them now as though they were mere acquaintances, shaking hands and completing the traditional verbal greetings. He tells them to fetch us some water and, when we settle down on a mat on the veranda, Saidou hands it to us without a word. They do not join us. With me they are also formal, and it was only when they were young that I managed to be more intimate with them. Now, they clearly do not want this. There is a strict code of conduct they are expected to adhere to, a code that requires complete deference to and respect for your elders. This can seem cold but there is nothing cold about Salif's family or their relationships with each other. The bright eyes and cheerful dispositions of the children do not speak of a respect based on fear or intimidation.

Salif is especially attentive to his children's upbringing, and the bonds in his immediate family are particularly strong. But it is not always like this. People often need to think a little before they can tell you how many children they have. They will rarely know their precise ages. When people refer to their 'parents' or 'brothers' and 'sisters', they could just as easily be talking about their cousins or uncles and aunts. In the same way that, in the traditional setting, individualism is transcended by the interests of the family, the dynamic of the wider family eclipses that of the more immediate ones. On the one hand, this creates a large enough unity to withstand significant pressures; on the other, it creates pressures of its own, where individuals and smaller families are unable to take the more spontaneous or autonomous decisions the modern world requires and a leaden inertia can take hold that makes even the simplest of actions difficult to initiate.

For the children, though, the security created by the unity of the larger family is immense. They may be treated with great strictness, frequently thwacked across the ear for misdemeanors and expected to fetch and carry for their elders at any moment, but the love they experience, particularly at a young age, from so many people is evident. The little posses that roam their compounds like renegade bands, playing with whatever bits and pieces they come across, can expect the same care from people in whatever part of the compound they go to. They may be naked, covered in dust and snot, have not a single personal possession to their name; they may be treated often little better than servants, have not a bed between them and be expected simply to sleep wherever they curl up; but they have a world of such loving boundaries that their freedom knows no limits.

Ibrahim Tandia, the development consultant Salif and I are to pick up today, is due to arrive in the afternoon, crossing as planned over the river from Senegal at the official border crossing adjacent to the town. Meanwhile, Amadou Tall, in near-constant mobile communication with Salif, is working on the problem of vehicle hire. We recover a little from our journey in Mamadou Kane's house, then go off to see a colleague.

Monsieur Méline, or Méline, as we know him, has a tiny, cubicle-sized office just around the corner from Mamadou Kane's. It's a long, thin, windowless room leading directly off a dusty street, just wide enough for his desk to span it at the far end. Méline is an agronomist. He has set up business as a consultant and has worked from time to time for a number of government agencies and European Union- or World Bank-funded programs. The walls of his office bear old posters showing the breeding cycle of the locust, or compost-making systems. His metal desk and accompanying filing cabinet spill with reams of paperwork. He has a fan but no computer. Two chairs sit before his desk, one without a back.

Méline rises graciously to greet us as we enter his office.

'Ah, welcome, welcome,' he says, his round, friendly face shiny with sweat. 'So... so... you have come...' He shakes his head, apparently overwhelmed with delight. 'Come, take a seat... please, please, be seated,' he says.

We take our seats and I ask him how business is.

'Ah... ah...' he exclaims, as though he has caught me out making a joke. 'Monsieur Peter...' he laughs. 'What business? You know how it is. Ask Salif. A little bit here; a little bit there. No-one has any money and the agricultural restructuring program people have been working on is in its second evaluation phase. Anyway, there is no work coming from that direction. It is foreign NGOs that give me the best chance of work. I

am just working on a tree-nursery proposal for a community group. It is not much. But what can you do?' he says, an apologetic smile on his face.

Méline has been struggling ever since I have known him. He runs a farmer-training program for us. This he does well, although there are a number of problems. We have also commissioned a few project studies from him, more perhaps than we should have. For the fact is, although Méline clearly knows his stuff agriculturally, he does not know much about project design. What he misses out in the simple details of who is going to do what, for whom and for what benefit, he makes up for in large amounts of irrelevant verbiage and budgetary micro-calculation. His reports are vast and nearly useless, and it is only his great enthusiasm and sincerity that persuaded me, perhaps against my better judgment, to give him such commissions. He is a man you cannot help liking. The fact is, most of the best-qualified development consultants are simply not to be found in towns such as this. They reside on high, internationally funded commissions in the capital, employed in producing the mountains of analyses and reports that consume such a high percentage of project budgets. They avoid rural areas like the plague.

Méline, apparently, does not go for this.

'What are they all doing in the capital?' he asks. 'This is where agronomists should be… in the countryside, where the real work is.' I suspect, not unreasonably, and given half the chance, however, he would not turn down a cushy job in the capital himself.

We have come to see Méline on a difficult matter. The training program he runs for us is going to be consumed by the larger community project we are working on, of which we are not expressly asking him to be a part. We do not mind if he takes a minor role in it, but we have another agronomist who will be in charge. I do not know how the situation stands and am happy to leave it up to Salif. But Salif is close on the matter. I do not know whether this is out of a certain feeling of loyalty to Méline, or because he too is feeling his way forwards.

'Méline can still run some of the training modules,' he told me before.

'And the training is to be structured differently, with more in-field work?' I asked.

'Yes. He could not do that.'

'Why not?'

'He would not want to. He does not have transport.'

'You don't think he would want to carry on with us?'

'He would like to, yes. But he's okay. Don't worry about Méline.'

This has left me little purchase, and I am uncertain what manner to adopt in our meeting with Méline. I leave it in Salif's hands. We chat amiably for a while but nothing as far as I can see is mentioned concerning the 'issue'. It is stiflingly hot, and again I am drooping. Salif tells Méline we have to go and see about hiring a vehicle, and we leave, having promised to pass the afternoon with him.

Amadou Tall has been on the mobile again. He has found a vehicle and driver. We go back to Mamadou Kane's and shortly he appears with two Moors, whom he introduces to us. One is Mustapha, the driver, a large man with a large black beard and the deepest of black eyes. The other is Harana, the vehicle 'boy', a pleasant, fresh-faced young man. Both wear *bobos* and turbans and seat themselves beside us on the mat with little formality. Salif speaks Hassaniya, the form of Arabic spoken by the Moors, and they enter 'discussions', mixing the Hassaniya up with French. These take considerable time, not helped by the fact that we want to pin down the exact details of what we require, when, for how long and how much it will cost, with all contingencies covered. Salif knows as well as I do how things can turn out otherwise.

'And no lifts – no extra passengers,' he says, anticipating

the habit of hire vehicles to double up as public transport when not expressly forbidden from doing so.

'No lifts. No problem,' Mustapha answers.

'And if we need the vehicle for extra days, we pay the same rate.'

'Same rate. No problem,' the Moor replies.

Even though Salif negotiates a price considerably lower than the one initially suggested, the cost is still very high. There is nothing we can do about this, as anything to do with vehicles is expensive in Mauritania. We will not pay mileage but will buy all fuel instead. Once this is concluded, the Moors stand up, shake our hands and depart. I realize we have not even seen the vehicle.

Salif's mobile phone seems to be almost permanently on the go. What with the two-day seminar starting tomorrow, the arrival of Ibrahim Tandia, and any number of issues concerning ongoing projects and his group's agricultural service delivery work, not to mention all sorts of family issues and the job he apparently has to perform as general post deliverer and money transfer agency for all and sundry, he has his work cut out. Often, indeed, I wonder how he manages and I am always pressing him to offload more of his responsibilities. The truth is, though, it is he, not anyone else, with whom people want to deal. The urge to turn his mobile off must be strong, but this he never does. How he managed before the advent of the mobile phone, I cannot remember.

The issue for the moment is just when and exactly where Ibrahim Tandia will arrive. Although he will be coming from Senegal, he is actually based in Germany, where he works for a German organic farming group. His expertise is in working with rural community organizations, and he comes highly recommended. He has travelled from a town in the middle of Senegal to the village of Dohley, on the remote and inaccessible northern border of that country. This is where we run our Dohley Women's Market Garden Project and it is these women who have kindly taken it upon themselves to receive him and dispatch him over the Senegal River to Kaédi. Communication with the Dohley women is not going well, however, their mobile signal being weak.

At around one o'clock we walk to Méline's house to pass the afternoon, as arranged. It seems to me that the hot season has arrived, as it is about as hot as I can remember, the air dense with heat, like a wall. It feels like I am swimming.

Méline inhabits one of the elegant, colonial-era bungalows on an old, wide boulevard. How he comes to be there, and whether he rents it or owns it, I do not know, but it is now in a state of almost total dilapidation, with Méline and his family living in it in a state of gentle penury. He welcomes us at the doorway of the bungalow compound and, seeing the dripping, weary state I am in, immediately suggests I take a bucket bath. This is a wonderful suggestion, and once the bucket has been produced, I disappear behind the tall wall of the toiletry area. Here there is a wooden stool and a plastic basket with a cake of soap and a flannel in it. I have become proficient at maximizing the use of a bucket of water, soaping myself up from head to toe and working down from the top, rinsing it all off again. Always I leave enough water for one final slosh. That moment, no matter how brief, when my head is immersed in the water, is one of the most luxurious I know. For the tiniest of seconds, I am inhaling the humid scent of a grand, tropical waterfall.

Feeling recovered and refreshed, I join Salif and Méline where they are spread out on a mat and cushions in the shade of a wall.

The most notable thing about Méline is the great incongruity between his own personal attributes of warmth and self-effacement and the fact that he has an exceptionally unpleasant son. Perhaps I have been lucky in the fact that I do not remember coming across unpleasant children in Africa before, but this boy, 12 or 13 years old, appears spoilt, rude and highly disrespectful in a way so entirely out of context that it is shocking. Salif and I have often spent time at Méline's and so have come across him before, but I always find it uncomfortable when he slouches over to us on a request from his father to perform some minor service, then argues insolently that he does not want to do it, even refusing sometimes. I feel for Méline then, being humiliated in front of guests, and I am curious always to see what Salif's reaction will be, as this could not be more different from the manner in which his own children behave. He, as expected, does his best to play the situation down, remarking perhaps that children will be children. But I can see that this lessens his respect for Méline. It is not so much that children do not misbehave in Mauritania. Like everywhere, they do. But the sneering insolence of this child towards his father is exceptional. No doubt there is a back-story.

Méline is a Kaédi man, born and bred. For me, the concept of living and existing in Kaédi holds a strange fascination. The town is so very run down and has so very little going for it. It is a rubbish tip with sporadic electricity, subject to the most crushing of heats, a heat that barely lets up the year round. The place feels pointless somehow; as though its creation during the colonial era was a mistake, as though it should never have been here. But here, too, of course, there is a back-story, one with a different perspective to this. I remember one evening Méline and Salif reminiscing about the town, talking of the old tennis courts there used to be out by the old parade ground, of the art-deco cinema, now a shell, and of the now non-existent park where, as students, they would take their books in the afternoons.

'It was something, then, this town,' Méline had said, and I realized then that he was not living in a rubbish tip. He was living in his hometown.

We eat, doze and drink tea. The issue of Méline's

continued employment – or not – is not raised. Perhaps an understanding has already been arrived at. I do not know, and Salif is not telling. When, later on in the afternoon, we leave, however, Méline mentions at the last moment, just as I am shaking his hand, that he is looking forward to the seminar tomorrow. I had not wanted to ask if he would be attending, imagining for some reason that he was not. I am glad that he is.

We are waiting for the call from the Dohley women to tell us that Ibrahim Tandia is on his way across the river. We return to Mamadou Kane's and soon Salif's mobile rings. It is the president of the Dohley Women's Co-operative. Salif can only just make out what she is saying. Ibrahim Tandia is on his way. He calls Mustapha, the driver of the hire vehicle, and tells him to come and pick us up. Shortly an engine can be heard revving outside the compound doorway. It is a handsome vehicle, thankfully in good condition: a more modern version of the same Toyota double-cabin pickup we have. Now commences an hour of confusion as the whereabouts of Ibrahim Tandia and the Dohley woman who is accompanying him – and who is in sporadic phone communication with us – becomes increasingly unclear. We make our way back and forth across town, negotiating dry riverbeds, passing through broken-down compounds and becoming stuck in an absurd 10-vehicle gridlock by the market. By the time we link up with them, all are hot and irritable.

Ibrahim Tandia inspires confidence the moment you meet him. He is sweating but not at all put out by the confusion that has seen him wandering about the hot streets of Kaédi, laughing at the situation and telling us to think nothing of it.

'These things happen,' he says.

He is middle-aged, a little portly, with an open face and engaging charm. He's wearing jeans and an endearingly crumpled safari hat, marking him out, along with me, in a street where everyone else is dressed in traditional clothes.

With Mohammed, Salif's eldest son, who is returning home, and Harana, the vehicle 'boy', in the back of the vehicle, we head out of town for the road back to Keniéba. Mustapha, our driver, now gives us a demonstration of how to go places. The main *piste* to Keniéba, many parts of which are now under construction into a tarmac road – a tarmac road that, a long 15 years in the coming, is now finally picking up speed on its journey to Keniéba – is avoided by most people because its surface is covered in corrugations so deep that it can destroy a vehicle in one journey alone. There is only one way to travel over the corrugations, and that is with speed. If a vehicle is travelling fast enough, its wheels simply skip from the top of one corrugation to the next, leading to a smooth ride. This, however, means that the vehicle's actual contact with the road is dramatically reduced, which leads to a good deal of 'drift'. When combined with the fact that every few kilometers we are required to come to a shuddering halt where a section of the *piste* is under construction or has been dissected by a *oued*, this can lead to an alarming ride. A hundred kilometers an hour seems about the minimum speed at which the road can be taken. Mustapha is in his element. Ibrahim Tandia, sitting up front, is unfazed. Leaning over to us in the back, a grin on his face, he shouts: 'We have a good driver. A true Mauritanian.' Not a flicker passes Mustapha's face. We reach Keniéba in just over an hour: a record.

Early evening: Mariam has laid out the mats and cushions. We settle down, Salif prone, exhausted; Ibrahim Tandia propped easily on an elbow, watching with small, smiling eyes all that takes place around us. The cattle and the goats and sheep are just arriving back from their day's browsing, and the compound for the moment is a farmyard. Two people have appeared. The first is Drémis, as he is called, a first cousin of Salif's, who comes over to greet us and shake our hands.

Drémis is the son of the old woman in the house next door who has lost the use of her legs; the elder brother of 'workshy' Mamadou. He is a former police officer. When I first met Drémis many years ago, he was a strong man. He was full of brash energy and wont to stomp around the compound ordering people about. No-one minded being ordered about by Drémis because he had a ready humor and was always prepared to back down. Over the years, though, I have seen him change. At first, people did not know what was wrong with him. He became paler and paler until his skin took on a pasty, grey texture. He had problems breathing and eventually went to the hospital in Nouakchott where tests were done and he was told that he had a heart condition, for which he was given medication. Recently, he has developed diabetes. Although still cheerful and robust in manner, today he is a shell of his former self.

'How are you?' I ask, as he shakes my hand.

'I am an old man now,' he says. 'Look at me.' And so he is. He is hunched, moves with a hobble and looks as though a strong gust of wind might blow him away.

Drémis's infirmities, however, I am aware, do not prevent him from remaining highly active in his love life. He has two wives in Keniéba, one at either end of town, and another, I have been told, about which the first two have no idea, in Nouakchott. How he affords these three wives and his many offspring – he himself cannot tell you how many he has – I have no idea, as he only does a small amount of clerical work now for the town mayor. Although it is not unusual for men to have more than one wife in Keniéba, it is not common, and the complexities of Drémis's marital arrangements afford the family a good deal of entertainment. Mariam is merciless. 'You are not old,' she says to him, 'just worn down by all those wives.'

'No, no,' Drémis replies, wagging his finger at her.

There is a dispensary in Keniéba but no other medical

facilities. Drémis is, in some respects, lucky in that he has managed to receive treatment for his condition. Most illnesses go untreated and people simply die. Entirely curable conditions such as jaundice or pneumonia are generally fatal.

Since I have been coming to the village, so many people have died, often the most unexpected ones: young people; those who, when I last saw them, seemed in the best of health. Each year there is a toll. Always it is 'the heart'. There is great sadness always, a sense of loss, and often the women can be heard wailing loudly in the town, as they are highly demonstrative on the death of a close one. But there is also acceptance.

'Life is a field we are set to work by Allah,' an old man once told me. 'Death is another of his fields.' There is little trauma in death.

One of the many who died between my trips – someone who, for some reason, stands out in my mind – is a young student I came to know in the town in the north of the country where Salif worked for the mining company before he returned to the village. I had gone up to stay with Salif in the house he inhabited in the whitewashed, purpose-built complex the mining company had constructed on a salt plain near the sea. This was a strange place but Salif and Mariam had a good life there, eating cheap fish fresh from ocean and forming close friendships with neighbors and colleagues. Their small apartment was something of a focal point for family members and always at night the lounge became a dormitory. Here I met Mohamedou, a tall, bright-eyed young man. He had just recently finished his *bac*, and was looking to further his education. He was full of plans and hopes. We would walk the nearby rubbish-strewn shore where the rusty carcasses of dozens of ships lay decaying, floundering in the shallows like beached whales or creating dark, cancerous shadows further out in the blue. He wanted to go to university: France, Dakar, Russia – anywhere would do. He was young, intelligent, ambitious, and, as we walked, he would tell me how he was waiting – waiting like all the other tens of millions of young Africans hoping for a better life.

'I cannot get a grant,' he said, 'so I am working, carrying fish in the market. I am trying to save money for a visa and a ticket.' He was full of hopes but it did not look to me as if he expected to fulfil many of them. Five years later, Salif told me he had died. He never made it to university, and was still living and working in the north when he became suddenly ill. As for what he died from, Salif could only give me the stock answer: the heart.

Working at the Mayor's office, Drémis, I know, will be busy helping to make arrangements for the elections, which are due shortly after I leave. I ask him how this is going.

'Ah,' he exclaims. 'The elections! Pah, pah, pah. So much to do. There are 74 parties and we have local elections as well. Very complicated.'

I remark on the number of parties, some of which I know have boycotted the elections.

'Each candidate must be very rich,' Drémis says. '*Very* rich,' he emphasizes. 'He will need millions, to provide great feasts for his supporters, and for many other things as well. That is the only way you can win elections here. You must throw a big party and make everyone happy.' Only half the population is eligible for voting, Salif has told me, the government long having been highly exclusive about who can apply for papers: if you've lost yours, or they're damaged, or you've just never got around to applying for them, which is not uncommon in rural areas, you're unlikely to get them, and particularly so if you are of the wrong ethnicity. Mariam has lost hers and has been unable to replace them.

The other person who has appeared in Salif's compound this evening is Alisanne. Alisanne is the younger brother of

Amadou, Salif's cousin in Nouakchott in whose rooms we lodged. It is luck that has brought him to Keniéba the same time I am here, as he lives and works in France and only comes home once every two years. By the same coincidence, I met him last time he was back and he has also visited my home in England. He comes over to greet us where we sit.

Alisanne is bright and friendly, with an easy charm. Stocky, with a shiny, open face, he is younger than me, although no longer the young man who set out for France 12 years previously. He is streetwise and clearly adept at 'working the system'. Where many millions of others wish and talk about making it to Europe, he, apparently, had no difficulty in doing so. And then, once there, in what seemed a very short time, not only had he acquired a council flat in Paris but also, only a short time later, a French passport. These accomplishments he brushes aside.

'Yes, I have a flat. Yes, I have a French passport,' he told me when I last met him. 'There are ways... you know...' It was only when pressed closer about this over the course of a few days that more details emerged. It had by no means been a simple task. He explained: 'Getting there was the most difficult. I went with some companions into the desert. There we paid some Arabs to take us into Algeria. They were not good men. They took our money, but they did not look after us. We did not have enough water, and the vehicle we were in broke down. We had to walk for many days. But we were lucky. I heard of others who were simply taken out into the desert and left to die.'

He made it across Algeria and into France, although he did not furnish details of how he accomplished this. Once in France, he dumped his passport and all means of identification.

'At that time you could get refugee status this way,' he said. 'You read the newspapers and saw where the wars were and told the immigration people you were from that country. To them all black people look the same. They gave you a temporary permit to stay in the country and provided accommodation for you.'

He spent a number of years working the system, gradually improving his official status until, after a sufficient number of years' residency, he was eligible for a French passport. At one period he lived and worked in Belarus. He told me how he would get there. 'It was well known that immigration officials did not bother first-class train passengers if they were asleep,' he said. 'So all you had to do was buy a business suit and a first-class train ticket, and when you came to the border pretend to be asleep.'

Alisanne makes it all sound easy, as that is his way, but I have seen the change that has come over him since he went away and I am aware of the stress and difficulty of being first-generation immigrants into the EU. Life for them is not easy. To those still in Africa, the West may resemble some sort of nirvana where jobs pay well and the standards of living are high. The reality is different. More often than not, first-generation immigrants end up living in the very poorest of housing estates among some of the most socially deprived communities, employed in factories paying the minimum wage, or not even that. The cost of living is exceedingly high; they are isolated; the weather is dreadful; and they have yet to become part of any constituency with sufficient influence to improve their status. On top of this, they must send money home. When Alisanne came to see me in England, I went to pick him up at the house of an acquaintance of his who resided in a housing estate on the edge of a large provincial town not far from where I live. Looking for the right house, I asked a neighbor if he knew the family.

'Fucking blacks,' is all the middle-aged, shaven-headed man replied.

The estate was of the most rundown variety and the flat was almost entirely devoid of furniture or possessions, with no curtains and only a vast television set in the living room. Alisanne's friend – a man from Sierra Leone – was charming and insisted I stay for something to eat. He worked in a nearby factory for the minimum wage, had three young children, and his wife was ill in hospital. When I asked about his rent, I was shocked at how high it was. This man was certainly not living in any sort of nirvana. Even if he had wanted to return to his home in Sierra Leone – and he told me this was his eventual ambition – the likelihood of its happening in the near future was low, as he did not have sufficient money to pay for the flights for all his family and anyway, he told me, there would probably be no work for him when he got there.

Alisanne did not hold a lot of sympathy for his friend, remarking only that he should look for a better job. Alisanne's own job, however, was not much better. Originally, he had worked the streets of Paris and Amsterdam, selling African trinkets and souvenirs. This was a good business for a young man with few responsibilities but, as life became more complicated and he married and found a flat, he moved on to construction sites. This was exceptionally hard work and, although it paid sufficiently, did not produce high rewards for unskilled labor. Years of this exhausted him, and it was during this period I saw the most significant change come over him. The strong young man I had once known became overweight, puffy-faced and stressed. The last time I saw him, he told me he had quit construction.

'I'm at the airport now,' he told me, as ever full of optimism. 'It's good there, although the wages are low.'

He was packing delivery vans for a courier company. Alisanne is bright and intelligent, and it occurred to me that he could get a better job than this. I asked him if he had been to job agencies; if he had looked for jobs in the service industries, for example. I was thinking at the least of a job in one of those many coffee-shop chains up and down the high streets. Surely he could move up from the bottom rung of the employment ladder. But Alisanne was strangely ambivalent about my suggestions.

'No, no. It's difficult,' is all he replied. I wondered how much of the difficulty was practical and how much was to do with a lack of confidence, with a mentality of self-imposed cultural ghettoization. When I probed gently about his life in France it seemed to confirm this. His expectations were low.

'Our life is simple,' he said. 'We work. We eat African foods at home with our wives and children. We go to the mosque to pray. On Sundays we visit our friends. We send money home. That is all. We are Africans,' he laughed, 'we do not need more.'

Alisanne lives in one of the poorest suburbs of Paris, one that a while ago was at the center of some riots. These were known locally as 'The Sons of the Immigrants Riots', as it was not the first-generation immigrants who participated in them but their more culturally liberated offspring. They caused considerable disruption across France. Alisanne was dismissive at the time.

'It's these young people,' he said. 'They do not know how to behave. They want everything without having to work for it.'

Life was not easy for Alisanne, I knew. But he would be the last to admit this. Back in the village he looks happy and relaxed. He greets me warmly, but he does not join us on our mats. 'I have many visits to make,' he says, giving me a wink. I know what those visits mean.

Darkness descends and the mêlée of livestock in the compound clears, the animals making their way to their pens at the far end. The air being a little cooler in the open space of the compound, away from the hot walls of the buildings, Mariam moves us and our mats and cushions further out into it. Here we settle down quietly, awaiting the evening meal. Ibrahim Tandia is clearly familiar with village life. Although he now lives in Germany and, I know, is from an urban background, he is at ease, happy to play with the young children who crawl over him like a giant teddy bear. A little later Mustapha, our driver, and Harana, his young colleague, appear. They, I can see, are a little ill at ease. They are Moors, and this compound in the old part of a Peul town in the heart of the south represents the home-base of Black African culture as much as anywhere. They have no animosity but a whole history of distrust and rivalry between the two communities cannot so easily be swept aside. Salif puts on a show of bonhomie, inviting them to sit down and cracking jokes. The Moors respond cheerfully enough, but their fear of being patronized is apparent.

'You'll eat,' Salif says. The Moors decline politely. 'Yes, surely... you'll stay to eat,' he insists. The Moors mumble their disinclination. 'My wife... she has cooked specially... she will be very angry.' The Moors smile. 'Wait... the food will be here soon.'

Mariam produces a great platter of heavily spiced macaroni to be eaten with bread, one of her specialities. The Moors take

a couple of handfuls each and get up.

'Eat, eat,' Salif insists, but the Moors are up, washing their hands from the *bidon*.

'*Bismillah*. We've eaten,' they say, backing away into the night.

I can see Ibrahim Tandia's eyes gleaming in the darkness.

'Good men,' he says as they depart. 'Good men.'

We lie and stare at the stars, which wink at us multitudinously. In other parts of the compound, groups mumble and stir to the dim glow of an oil lamp or faded beam of a torch. The livestock shift, with the odd explosive passing of air. In between each star are thousands – millions – of others. It is as if there is no blackness at all.

The children have fallen asleep, some curled on the sand, some at our feet, a couple draped over Salif. Mariam is rough with them. The smaller ones she picks up and deposits like sacks of potatoes on the mat by the house door. The others she shakes and pinches to wakefulness: 'Move, move. Wake up. Wake up,' she bullies them. They stagger drunkenly over to the mat where they curl up in a line, their hands pinched between their knees like fetuses.

6 The Seminar

Ethnic complications... A splendid array... Three-way translation... The Moor's protest... A gender lesson... The expert conductor finds an assistant... A memorable journey... A little country banditry... The virtues of compost

It is the first day of the seminar and Ibrahim Tandia is up early. We eat a quick breakfast, then he, Salif and I are off across town to the *Centre*.

Paying for a consultant to come to Mauritania is something of a long-shot. We have never done anything like this before and are eager to see how it will turn out. We were aware only of the importance of the seminar and the necessity of having someone with sufficient experience and authority to lead it.

Salif and I have been wondering for some time how we might create a project that was truly inclusive of the many ethnic and cultural groups in the region. For, in the region near to Keniéba where we conduct our work, there is a large and complex mix, one that has taken me the longest time to untangle. First, there are the Moors, mostly the Black Moors, or Harratin, those descended from freed slaves. Then there are the White 'Arab', or *Bidan* Moors – those more directly descended from the Yemeni Arabs who came south in the 17th century and the Berbers who were already in the region – who are mostly, but not entirely, concentrated further north. Then there are the Bantu Black African peoples, who come mainly from the Peul and Soninke ethnic groups and within whose numbers, as with the Moors, there are further divisions along caste lines. The Peul are a part of the greater Fulani people, traditionally a pastoral, cattle-breeding group, but also a people who, over the centuries, have settled in many towns, gaining reputations for learning, conducting trade and forming powerful states of their own. They are often fairer skinned and more aquiline than other West Africans and some hold a tradition that they originated in southern Egypt. In Mauritania, as elsewhere, the Peul are Muslims, as are their compatriots, the Moors. This, however, has not prevented the history of rivalry and conflict between the two communities that continues to this day.

All these ethnic and social groupings are further divided along occupational lines, such as pastoralists, commercial irrigation farmers, small-scale vegetable growers and traditional farmers. And then there is the gender divide. Across all these groups, the needs of the women differ from those of the men.

Would it be possible to devise a project inclusive of all these diverse groups? If so, it could only help to create some much-needed harmony across the community. It is with this in mind that Salif has spent the last year travelling around the countryside canvassing all the different groups, talking to them about our plans and motivating them to voice their opinions. This has not been easy, as the lack of cross-community collaboration as well as the absence of any cultural precedent for the sort of analytical approach required do not lend themselves to acceptance of a new approach. Of course, there has long been collaboration of sorts between communities, such as the tradition for pastoralists, Moorish or otherwise, to graze their livestock on crop residues, with payment being in the form of the animal manure that then fertilizes the farmers' fields. And for centuries farmers and animal herders have been innovating, adapting their practices to changing climatic or market contexts.

In recent decades, though, the rate of change has been exceptional. The rains are consistently so poor now, for example, that, in order to achieve sufficient water penetration of the soil, many farmers group together to hire tractors to plough their fields; grazing pastures so quickly become exhausted that pastoralists have to travel further and further to find them; and due to the vagaries of markets the world over – markets that are slewed by the neoliberal economic policies and the subsidized efficiencies of the rich world – the prices for cash crops are often so bad that they do not cover costs. Even in the extreme conditions of today, however, there are solutions – solutions we hope Ibrahim Tandia is going to help the farmers discover and develop.

The simple fact of having the seminar is in itself a significant movement in this direction. The desired outcome – consensus on the shape and design of a project – is almost a bonus. The mere fact of having motivated and organized people sufficiently to all come together on one particular day in one particular place for one particular purpose already indicates some degree of success.

So, as Ibrahim Tandia, Salif and I march towards the *Centre*, files and briefcases business-like under our arms, we do so with a sense of confidence and excitement. We are cheerful and optimistic. There will be as many as 150 people present, representing some 35 co-operatives and groups across all sectors of the community. This is the theory.

We reach the door of the compound and, amazingly, not only is there not a single person there, the door is actually locked and Salif does not know where the key is. It is a bad moment. Ibrahim Tandia folds his arms, looking mildly amused. Salif looks embarrassed. I struggle to contain my frustration. Frantic phone calling from Salif ensues. Then he goes off. Ibrahim Tandia and I sit down in the shade of the compound wall.

'They will learn,' Ibrahim Tandia says. 'If they want to modernize, if they want to lift themselves up, they will learn to respect time.'

We sit and wait, and a group of women arrive. Later, some men show up. Later still, Salif reappears with the key, unlocks the metal doors of the *Centre* compound and opens up the main room of the building. People drift in while we arrange chairs, and Ibrahim Tandia sets up a blackboard. We are cheerful again now. Méline is here from Kaédi, as are a number of Keniéba dignitaries. All is coming together, not perhaps as Ibrahim Tandia and I in our efficient, Western way would have liked, but in an African way. It is happening, but slowly. The constituent parts of a complex organizational maneuver are slowly gelling and, before long, there is a great crowd and a loud babble of voices.

The room is large and spacious and chairs have been brought in from all over the town. Everyone is dressed up in their best. All are encouraged to sit, either on mats on the floor or on the chairs. Here, to one side, the women, resplendent in voluminous dresses, are given chairs. In the front row, the town mayor, the local member of parliament and a number of elders look important and impressive in brilliant white *bobos*. Farmers, pastoralists, commercial rice producers: they are all here. Some are bright-eyed and switched-on, some wary, some tall and handsome, some gnarled; many display fine examples of the wide range of bodily ailments so prevalent in rural areas: bald eyes, twisted legs, crazily dysfunctional teeth, severe skin diseases. There are Moors, but only a few, and a great many familiar faces.

Salif starts proceedings by thanking all for coming and calling on the Mayor to speak. The Mayor is a tall, gruff man. He does not stand, but bellows out a traditional speech in which all are thanked for their invaluable participation and Allah is invoked for his blessings.

Next, the local MP rises. Monsieur Tissalou is a large, expansive, white-haired man in the traditional African 'Big Man' mould. Utilizing a well-practised manner, he delivers a long, mesmeric speech that leaves everyone in no doubt as to his magnanimity. He finishes on a useful and valid point.

'We are not all the same. We are not all as one. This is the nature of community: the coming together of peoples of differing castes and tribes and cultures. But does this hinder us? No, it does not. Does it prevent us achieving our aims? No, it does not. Messieurs Salif, Peter and Tandia have come here to assist us. For that, we must thank Allah. All that is done is His work and is done in the light of His benevolence. Allah is our guide and Father. We must all humble ourselves before His great magnificence. And now to end: my part in these proceedings is small and insignificant. I am not here as a participant but only to welcome our guests and give my blessings on your endeavors. But I have one suggestion before I go. Messieurs Peter and Tandia speak French. Already we have translation into Peul. There has been some attempt at translation into Hassaniya for our Arab friends. But I suggest we be more organized about this. I think, Monsieur Salif, for the sake of harmony and equality, translators could be selected and pauses made in all verbal correspondence in order to allow time for every person in the room to understand what is being said. That is all I have to say. My part is done. Soon, indeed, there are elections and I may be an MP no more. But in the meantime, may Allah bless these proceedings with success and harmony.'

Applause commences as Monsieur Tissalou takes his seat, nodding his appreciation about him. A great discussion ensues, resulting in official translators being selected. Everything that is now said is translated three ways: into French, Peul and Hassaniya.

It is now time for Ibrahim Tandia to take the floor. In a more business-like manner, he thanks all for coming and

quickly gets down to explaining the format and objectives of the next two days. Monsieur Tissalou, the MP, cannot restrain himself and every few minutes applauds Ibrahim Tandia and commends him on what he has said, often expanding on this theme for some considerable time. Ibrahim Tandia does not betray the slightest sign of impatience at these interruptions, but calmly continues on from where he left off once free to do so. Presently a question comes from the back.

'Where is the representation from the Moorish community?'

Ibrahim Tandia looks to Salif.

'Uh, we have a number of that community here,' Salif says.

'We are many and there are only two or three here,' the voice calls out. A small, wiry 'White' Moor with an impish face pushes himself forwards.

'I spoke to Ould Barka and Ould Talabaye yesterday,' Salif says, 'and they said they would be here. We also have a number of Harratin present.'

'This is nothing,' the man says, apparently dismissing the

Black Moor Harratin community in one fell swoop. 'What kind of meeting is this that each community is not represented properly? When benefits come to this community, all should get their fair share. Why is this white man here? He is here to help us all. Whatever he has to give us is for all, not just for certain people. It is a disgrace. I say...'

By now such an uproar has broken out in the room that it is difficult to hear what the Moor is saying. People are shouting and arguing. The Moor is putting on a display of great indignation. Ibrahim Tandia is unfazed and just stands there, his arms folded. Salif is trying to reason with people, to no effect. The dignitaries in the front row, including Monsieur Tissalou, who so recently had the crowd eating out of his hand, look impotent.

'We are all represented fairly... everyone was told about the meeting... let the man speak... are they giving out fencing materials?... when's lunch?' people are shouting. One man roars at the Moor: 'They are giving nothing away for free so you can go now.' Another, to great hilarity, shouts: 'The lamb will be here soon. Don't miss the meal.'

The Moor is hopping up and down. He shouts: 'This is nothing. This meeting is nothing.' He stalks to the door. 'It is nothing,' he yells over his shoulder as he departs.

The babble of talk and shouting goes on for some time but gradually subsides as Salif calls all to order. 'Our friend is free to leave if he wishes,' he says when he can finally be heard. 'Let Monsieur Tandia continue.'

Ibrahim Tandia takes up his theme again and, before long, is tying up his introduction. The Mayor and Monsieur Tissalou take this opportunity, along with most of the elders, to depart. Now the seminar can start in earnest. What has passed so far is both an indication of the challenge faced by this disparate, unruly community and of the usefulness of such meetings in creating the space in which steam can be let off. Ibrahim Tandia highlights this at the start of the first seminar session.

'We are here to voice our opinions. Everyone – even those with the strongest opinions,' he says with a smile, 'is welcome to speak out.'

Ibrahim Tandia's first objective, he tells us, is to get people to think about themselves and their communities under the four topic headings of Strengths, Weaknesses, Opportunities and Threats; in other words, to conduct what, in development jargon, is known as a SWOT analysis. This he does unashamedly by splitting the group up along gender lines. He winks at Salif and me as the groups separate.

'You will see what happens,' he says.

The men all crowd outside where, for 45 minutes, a great uproar can be heard. The women stay in the room and settle down, quietly discussing the issues with one of their number elected to record the results. After the allotted time, Ibrahim Tandia calls all back to the room and writes the findings of each group down on the blackboard. It is a joke. The men have managed to record only three bare facts: they need fencing materials; they need wells; and they need seed. The women, on the other hand, have come up with all sorts of details about themselves and the environment in which they live. Strengths consist of sun, good soil, water from the river and available labor. Weaknesses consist of broken equipment, lack of transport, crop pests and poor availability of agricultural inputs such as fertilizer and seed. Opportunities include a ready market for vegetables and the possibility, they hope, for the project to provide them with literacy classes. And the threats consist of desertification and environmental degradation.

'You see,' Ibrahim Tandia says to the gathering, 'the womenfolk do not only have the beauty, they have the brains as well.'

'It is not just for making babies that we are good,' a young pregnant woman shouts out to more laughter.

Ibrahim Tandia is a master at his trade. Throughout the morning I watch him stimulate and then harness the potential of the delegates. How he does this is a mystery, as he never imposes himself or gives opinions. He is like a conductor. At his hands gradually the crowd harmonizes, potential leaders, thinkers and innovators emerging as if by gravity. His technique may involve traditional developmental tools, but it is his charm and presence that produce the results. By the time we break for lunch in the early afternoon, working group leaders have been chosen, and there is an aura of excitement in the air. We are all tired and hot, yes – the temperature in the crowded room must be 45 degrees at least – and in need of some sustenance, but we have a gleam in our eyes. Any doubts I may have had about bringing in Ibrahim Tandia are washed away.

There has been activity in the *Centre* compound all morning preparing a great feast for the seminar delegates. Various members of Salif's family have set up a kitchen there, and large quantities of couscous have been cooked and two sheep slaughtered. Mamadou, Salif's cousin – he with the unsubstantiated reputation for being work-shy – is in charge and, when I popped out earlier in the morning for a breath of air, I found him gleefully up to his arms in sheep's blood, stripping the two hanging carcasses down with an expertise that made it look as if he were undressing them.

'We will feast well today,' he says, grinning happily.

Despite the promise of this, the seminar delegates have sensibly decided that, instead of passing the afternoon in a long drawn-out period of gluttony followed by a single evening seminar session, they will stop only briefly to eat and then crack straight on with proceedings. This will allow them to fit two further sessions in today which, along with two tomorrow morning, will complete the seminar, so giving them plenty of time tomorrow afternoon to regain their homes before nightfall. Everyone is happy with this decision, which, on the one hand, reduces the seminar length by half a day and, on the other, reflects people's enthusiasm for what is taking place, for there is nothing people like better than a long afternoon of eating. That they are giving up what may have been the primary motivation for many of them in coming is a tribute to Ibrahim Tandia's skill.

And so lunch is taken, in the shockingly short time of an hour, just long enough for people to say their prayers, stretch their legs and gather around the great steaming platters of meat and couscous. This is a popular, traditional meal, the couscous being made from the flour of millet, the staple crop, with the meat, consisting seemingly mostly of ribs, stomach lining and internal organs, piled high on top of it. People relish the food, cracking the bones and sucking out the marrow, helping each other twist stubborn joints in two, crunching gristle between their teeth. Tea is being made so that, immediately subsequent to the last mouthful, as tradition dictates, a glass can be had to 'wash the mouth'. And then we are back to work.

The afternoon session is as successful as the morning. A couple of further exercises are carried out, this time with the delegates broken down into more homogenous groups. There is one man who particularly stands out. He is a pastoralist with a wide, bright face and a halo of wild hair. What is most remarkable about him, however, is his intelligence and dynamism. I ask Salif who he is, and he tells me that he is simply a Peul livestock herder from a village a little to the north. Quickly this man emerges as a spokesperson, and it is not long before he is assisting Ibrahim Tandia in almost every facet of the seminar. His grasp of its subtleties is profound, as though he too had gained his doctorate in development studies.

'Monsieur Tandia, do you not think it would be good if you got the groups to mix a little,' he suggests in his good

French at one time. 'Perhaps group leaders could swap places for an exercise.'

At another time, when everyone is looking tired and lethargic, he has us all standing up doing arm-waving exercises. Whether he has come across this technique on some previous training program I do not know, but he has everyone in stitches, which wakes us all up. 'It is good, is it not?' he cries out as he swings his arms, a wild look in his eyes.

We break late in the afternoon, and everybody goes their own way, some to walk back to their villages, most to stay in town. Only a small group of irrigation farmers remains behind. It may already have been a long day, and we are all hot, but Ibrahim Tandia wants to visit their irrigation schemes. Salif, Méline and I are happy to accompany him.

The Moshe River, fed by 52 streams, is the water source for all irrigation in the region. Some 40 kilometers to the east of Keniéba, the river is dammed at a natural convergence of two lines of hills. All but eight of the streams feed into the river upstream of the hills, meaning the dam and its lake capture by far the larger part of the local water resource. The streams that feed the river are seasonal and are dry for most of the year. This is not the case for the Moshe, though, as the dam, along with another at its far end where it joins the Senegal River, guarantees a permanent supply of water. It is this that allows for irrigation farming in what is otherwise such a very dry region.

The Moshe is a small river some 20 to 30 meters across, depending on the season. It wends its way westwards across the Sahelian plain with thorny vegetation hugging its banks. It is where it approaches Keniéba, about halfway down its course, that it is most utilized. Here, much of the land in proximity to it, if not entirely above its flood plain, is of high enough elevation at least to reduce the risk of flooding. In all, there are some 70 private irrigation schemes down the length of the Moshe, covering around 3,000 hectares and benefiting, directly or indirectly, as many as 40,000 people from 50 villages or hamlets. Keniéba takes the lion's share of this, although the reality is that this agricultural sector functions exceptionally badly, with as much as half the land under the schemes either abandoned or exploited so poorly that it produces very little.

We are cheerful in the Toyota as we head out of town to inspect the irrigation schemes, Salif, at the last moment, having made his obligatory phone call to the adjutant. The sun is low, and there is a crowd of people in the back and many more squeezed into the cab. Mustapha, our driver, has a look on his face not unlike that of a camel: dignified and disapproving.

There is only one bridge over the Moshe and it is here at Keniéba. It crosses the river just outside town at a point where the river is at its widest with a long sandy slope running down to its edge. This is a busy spot, as it is to here that livestock herders from far and wide bring their beasts to water. Great herds of sheep, goats and cattle mill about, some just arriving, some held back a little distance until there is more space at the water's edge. The cattle wade in and stand motionless, sucking up draughts of the water. The sheep and goats line the shore, heads bowed. A little further up are a few camels, their long necks bent to their reflections, their nomadic, Moorish owners squatting beside them splashing water up their long, pale arms. A little aside, knots of women work away at large basins of washing, rinsing their materials in the river and joining forces to twist them dry before wending their way like ants back up the path to town, their washing balanced on their heads. Next to the washerwomen, bare-breasted girls soap themselves up whilst a little further out boys gallivant in the water, naked and lithe, like sprites. Despite the heat, I have never seen anyone other than these boys immerse themselves in the river for the sole purpose of cooling off. The only exception to this was one time when Salif, slowly and surprisingly, simply walked fully clothed into a deep part of the river, ducked his head under twice and walked back out. He was dry within half an hour.

We cross the bridge, and the *piste*, or elevated dirt track, runs straight as a die into the distance. For the longest time, my experience of the geography of this region was restricted to the few details I could glean from my large-scale map of Mauritania and whatever parts of it could be reached by donkey-cart, for those were the days before we had a vehicle of our own. Much time was passed rumbling over the plains to the plod of animal traction. Although this allowed me to gain an intimate knowledge of the immediate surroundings of Keniéba, it prevented me from grasping the larger context of a region where even small villages can be 15 kilometers apart. This road, for example, disappearing so enticingly to the distance, had always remained a mystery. I longed to travel down it, to open up the next page in the geographic story; to make it over the next horizon. Always, there seemed some reason preventing me from devoting the time to hitching a lift or taking transport down the road. But then, some years back, a perfect opportunity presented itself. Amadou, Salif's cousin back in Nouakchott, was on a mission to a town 70 kilometers east of Keniéba for his employer, the Department of Water and Hydrology. Returning to Keniéba one evening, we found Amadou installed *en route* for the night with a Toyota, driver and assistant. He was leaving early the next morning, and Salif and I were welcome to join him.

It was the end of the dry season, and the rains had been particularly bad that year. The countryside was burnt and desiccated, and the few cattle we passed as we set out from Keniéba looked emaciated and seemingly ready to drop. Their tall Peul herders, whom we left in our dust, did not look much better. Our driver, Barak, was a jovial man with whom Amadou, sitting up front, kept up an almost continual banter. Amadou himself was in good form. This for him was like a holiday. When I asked him what the mission was, he laughed. 'Just some Prefect up to tricks,' he said.

Barak, the driver, took the road at the requisite corrugation-defying speed, and the 'assistant', Moktar, an older man with a round, cheerful face, chanted what sounded like Qur'anic psalms, but the laughter certain sections created made me suspect were not. Salif was at ease, enjoying being liberated for the moment from any responsibilities.

We headed east and the countryside seemed, if possible, to become dryer, a black, gravelly rubble taking over from the scant pastures. Here, surprisingly, there were a number of tiny villages: desperate-looking collections of shanty-like huts isolated on the windswept plains. A few dazed-looking children stood about; perhaps an old man or woman, but otherwise no-one was visible. I asked Amadou how on earth they survived in such a barren spot.

'They have crops in the *oueds*,' he said. 'A few sheep? Who knows?' He sounded uninterested in these impoverished people but when, a little later, we passed a group of young boys carrying rocks to the side of the road in one of the many places where it had been partially washed away, he told Barak to pull over.

'What are you up to?' he called to the wide-eyed boys.

'We are building up the roadside,' they stammered. 'The road workers give us money for doing it.' At this, Amadou roared with laughter.

'Little bandits,' he said. 'Why should they give you any money? It was probably you who took the rocks away in the first place.'

The boys smiled shyly. 'Bandits,' he laughed again, shaking his head, 'genuine little bandits.' And the boys laughed too, as they could tell Amadou was being friendly. He told Barak to move on but, before we did, he dug his hand into his pocket and pulled out a handful of coins. 'Goodbye, little ones,' he called, scattering the coins on the ground as we pulled away.

Not long after this, I was surprised by a range of considerable hills appearing ahead of us. This was something new to me. Used to the flat monotony of southern Mauritania, I was quite unprepared for this. Soon the road was picking its way through a broken, rocky terrain. The hills looked old: ridges of black, cracked rock protruding like an old man's bones through the surface of the earth. The road was quite incapable of dealing with all this hardness and made no attempt to smooth a passage through the pass up to which we were headed. We were reduced to a crawl as we lurched over the rocks, turning steeply up the final hairpin. And then there before us was a magnificent view, one I had never before been afforded in Mauritania, the view of a distance only height can allow: a gently undulating plain of dry, yellow savannah stretching to such a very finite distance, with not a fence, town, person or any other mark of man visible, that it brought home to me with a sudden jolt a knowledge of the aboriginal heritage of the earth; that all was once unfenced; that the earth was once far bigger than humankind.

We swept down into that land, our spirits high, laughing for no apparent reason, and arrived a surprisingly short time later in the small town of Mbaye, which had been invisible from the pass. If the view from the pass had given rise in me to feelings of the sublime, Mbaye could not have been better constructed to provide the antidote. It was a desperate, forgotten, ignored, end-of-the-earth sort of place where people had left a not very edifying mark. A single, wide street lined with near-empty shops adjoined a shanty of wood and corrugated iron. At one end of town were the police and military posts, the school and the Prefect's residence. At the other, a wide *oued* planted with thin crops and traversed by the long elevation of the *piste*. The population looked threadbare and dejected. There were no vehicles except, amazingly, a single Toyota pickup converted into a Winston Cigarette advert that cruised slowly, as though in a Western, down the empty main street blasting an advert through its loudspeaker. Dust and drifts of plastic blew after it.

We drove through and out the other side to where the pumping station was situated beside the *oued*. Here, in a tangle of palms, a small shack containing the municipal pump was linked to a borehole in the middle of the dry riverbed. Amadou disappeared into the shack, only to reappear a few minutes later. We sped off to the Prefect's residence where he again disappeared. Later I saw him emerge to one side of the building. He was talking to a tall, well-dressed man, evidently the Prefect. The Prefect was animated, gesticulating with his arms. He turned abruptly on his heel and walked off. Amadou came over. He was smiling but remarked only: 'Imbecile.'

We went back to the main street in town and located the only shop that boasted a fridge, beside which we installed ourselves on the floor. The shop was basic, just a rough wooden counter and a single stack of shelves containing a few basic items. The owner was a friendly, intelligent-looking man, fatigue etched onto his face. We drank Fantas and waited.

The problem, apparently, was that the town pump had been reported as not running properly, but, in order to verify this, Amadou needed to replace the water-flow counter with a new one so that he could be sure the readings were correct. He needed the Prefect's permission to do this but the man had argued that this was not necessary. He had told Amadou he would come with him to the pump later. We waited an hour and half, then Amadou went back to the Prefecture, only to be told that the Prefect was in a meeting and could not see him. He returned to the boutique.

'I will put the new counter on anyway,' he said and disappeared with Barak and the Toyota.

'He'll need two hours to get a good reading,' Moktar, Amadou's assistant, remarked. A large woman now joined us on the floor of the shop and started making tea. It was stupefyingly hot, and I was not feeling well, but the lady was jolly and the banter between her, Moktar and the shop owner was lively. When, later, Amadou and Barak returned, they had with them some roasted meat in brown paper, and we set up a veritable picnic in the shade by the road outside the shop. It was dusty, sweaty and unbearably hot, but we were cheerful as we ate the meat with bread, drank new Fantas and washed all of this down with the large woman's teas.

Amadou was entirely unfazed by his standoff with the Prefect. 'He does not want us to install a new meter,' he said, 'because he has been making a profit from the water rates, charging his constituents one rate but having to submit a lower one because the meter is recording lower usage.' And, sure enough, when later we returned to the pumping station, he confirmed that the old counter had either malfunctioned or been tampered with.

'Just a little country banditry,' he remarked dismissively as we left.

The dam on the River Moshe was only a short distance from Mbaye, so, before starting our return journey, we made a detour to see it. It was a tall construction plugging a natural gap where two long lines of hills met. Behind was a vast and astonishing lake. To see so much water in this barren landscape was eerie, and we stood on the dam a little speechless, as none of my companions had seen this sight before either. Dead trees protruded from the surface of the water, indicating that it was not very deep. Looking at the lake reminded me why the storage of water in this way can be so contentious. Already, farmers must pay to take water which once came to them free with the floods after the rains, and whole communities' livelihoods are prey not only to political or economic exploitation, but also, and more likely, to mismanagement. It is not infrequent that whole crops are swept away by surges of water, when co-ordination between upper and lower dams fails.

It was not until some years later that I completed the geographic picture of this region, when I took the road to its conclusion at the far southern tip of Mauritania, near the Malian border. This was a one-way trip, as I was headed for Bamako, the Malian capital, from where I would fly home. Watching the country change from the barrenness of Mauritania to the comparative pastoral softness of Mali was fascinating. In fact, the northerly parts of western Mali that we were travelling through were dry, regarded as semi-desert themselves, but travelling south from Mauritania it did not feel like this. The villages seemed pretty and archetypal of agrarian African life, with round thatched huts, large shady trees and old men sitting peacefully in the shade of lean-tos. The people were colorful and healthy-looking and busy always: in the surrounding village fields, or ferrying mounds of produce to market on donkey-carts, or playing games of football on dusty patches of ground. How very different this was to the sparse existence that clings to the desiccated plains further north in Mauritania! It brought home to me how very difficult life was for people in Mauritania, and how very skilled they were in adapting to it.

'Those fields belong to Daouda Dirana,' Méline shouts from the front of the Toyota where he is squeezed next to Ibrahim Tandia as we cruise slowly up the *piste*. It is late afternoon, the seminar is over for the day and we have come to look at the irrigation schemes.

Méline indicates a large area stretching away to our right. 'He has 150 hectares,' he says, still shouting over the noise of the vehicle as it rumbles over the rough ground. 'But he only grows rice. That is the preferred cash crop because people think it is easy and will always fetch a good price. What they don't factor in is the high cost of diesel for the pumps and the cost of fertilizer.'

'How many hectares does he actually work?' Ibrahim Tandia asks.

'Not more than 30,' Méline replies, and explains how the scheme was part of a southern agricultural regeneration program funded by one of the large financial institutions active in Mauritania. Some $150,000 were spent on the land, he tells us, and Daouda Dirana was supposed to pay back a third of it.

'Why are they working so little land, then?' Ibrahim Tandia asks as we draw to a halt.

'The work that was done on the land was of such poor quality,' Méline says, 'that much of the terrain is not level enough for irrigation. Those responsible for implementing the works took half the money for themselves, meaning a proper job was not done. Meanwhile, Daouda Dirana is an old man and no-one cares whether he repays his share of the loan or not. Once he dies,' Méline says, 'the problem will be gone.'

A little further down the road is another large scheme:

190 hectares this time, with again only a small portion of it actually being worked. The story here though, Méline tells us, is a mixed one: a large amount of money was borrowed from the bank to set up the scheme, which then made a good start with a couple of good harvests. Then three years of disasters – a breakdown, a flooding and an insect invasion – meant they had to borrow more money from the bank.

'Sixty families take plots within this scheme,' Méline says, 'so many will suffer if it collapses. One good year, though, and they will be all right.'

We drive on and enter a gateway. The scheme here – 60 hectares of rice, vegetables and fruit trees – belongs to a family with wealthy connections and was one of the first to be set up in the region. I have been here a number of times and have always found the manager a little difficult. Moktar is tall and gruff, the younger brother of the *patron* who financed the scheme.

'Peasant agriculture… it's nothing,' he said, dismissing my praise of the well-organized scheme the first time I visited it. On another occasion, when I asked about his extensive banana plantation, he only laughed: 'Bananas are difficult. They are like children. They require a lot of time and money, then turn out bad.'

But in truth Moktar is a good farmer and a hard-working one; only, one suspects, a little frustrated at being a farmer rather than a man of wealth and influence like his brother. Ibrahim Tandia has no difficulty in charming him, inspiring him to give us a guided tour of his land. In one area we come across a plantation of fruit trees, next to each of which is a small metal plaque recording its name and variety. Moktar tells us that the trees were planted 10 years ago and are part of a research project the Agricultural Research Office was financed to conduct.

'They've come back to see them just once, though,' he laughs, 'and that was only because they had a film crew with them.'

Over the years I have visited many of the irrigation schemes in the Keniéba region. Generally somewhere between 5 and 25 hectares, these schemes are mostly owned by people who have risked everything to make the necessary investment. Usually, the owners have borrowed money from the banks to pay for the large water pumps and for the initial earthworks. As with the large scheme we saw earlier, the owners then mostly struggle to repay the loans, hampered, like Mabafé, Salif's family's scheme, by any number of problems. This year the issue is birds. From morning until night, people stand in their fields rattling cans to shoo away the huge flocks; some farmers, I've been told, have lost as much as two-thirds of their crops. The courage of these small, commercial farmers never ceases to amaze me. Year after year, they persevere, despite often seeing years' worth of work come to nothing, often going hungry in the process. They have no support and generally very little appropriate agricultural knowledge.

One man I have been visiting for many years has each year a new tale of disaster to relate. Musa is bright and cheerful but, according to Salif, not a particularly good farmer. On 'adventure' somewhere in West Africa as a younger man, as it is known when young men go off abroad in search of work, he returned home to Keniéba, he told me, 'because there was nothing for me there, whereas here we can grow food.' I find him always in the midst of his fields, a smile

of welcome on his face. He is always optimistic, always enthused.

'Not a bad year,' he'll say. 'But next year... next year, God willing, next year will be good.' One year, right in the middle of such a conversation, Musa suddenly hot-footed it away from me across his fields and out of view. A moment later, a vehicle turned up.

'Bank men,' Salif said.

We have time to visit only one further scheme, one we have helped develop so that it can be used as an example of good practice for others to see and copy. Already the sun has set, and the sky is crimson as we make our way to it. An individual for whom Salif obviously has a lot of respect runs the scheme. Mohamedou Samba is a tall, intelligent, gentle man dressed in a plain farmer's tunic. He takes us around his well-tended fields, explaining in good French all the things he has done. Fencing, he tells us, is his main problem, since here, as across much of the Sahel, enclosure of arable land is a big issue. In one part of the scheme we come across a number of compost pits – an innovation we have introduced – and Ibrahim Tandia asks our host what results he has had using the compost.

'I have used it on all my vegetables,' Mohamedou Samba says, 'and the yields are up 30 per cent.' Using controlled test plots, Salif and he have shown that the use of compost can also increase rice yields by 20 per cent. Getting other farmers to follow this example, though, will not be easy. Inspired and financed by certain powerful international institutions and foundations who believe in the concept of an agricultural sector based on the increased use of chemical fertilizers, the government has been handing out sacks of such fertilizer, free for the moment but of course only temporarily so.

We see the promotion of this new 'Green Revolution', as this global movement of new agricultural intensification based on the increased use of external inputs is termed, only putting agricultural production more and more into the hands of the few large transnational corporations that already control so much of the food production chain and which will naturally provide all these inputs. Next it will be genetically modified (GM) seed and all the products that must go with them on which farmers will necessarily become dependent, for each year all seed must be repurchased and each year, due to weakening soil fertility and pest and fungal immunity, more of the linked products will be required. In this manner, before long, if we are not careful, all food production, even at the most basic level, will be balanced on the volatilities and vagaries of a corporate global economic and political system not known for its robustness, sustainability or fairness. This is without even mentioning the vulnerability of such farming systems, with their poor soils and lack of adaptability, to climate change.

All of this Ibrahim Tandia, an internationalist, a wise man and an agronomist, knows well. Digging his hand now into Mohamedou Samba's compost pile, he extracts a handful of the rich, dark earth. Brandishing his fist aloft, his grinning face crimson in the evening light, he cries: 'Brown gold. Behold!'

It is dark by the time we make it back to town. Here the quiet of night quickly envelops us on our mats under the stars. We sit and await our evening meal, which does not appear until nearly midnight. Mariam, it seems, is in no hurry tonight.

7 The Life of the Compound

A moment of triumph... Child's play... Magnificent display... A battle with Polisario... Visions of paradise... Animal attitudes and the need for trees... The Peace Corps volunteer... Is the tractor necessary?... Ibrahim's plan

I wake in the night. All is still. Somewhere far off a donkey brays. Nearer to, a baby cries: not a full-throated wail, but a quieter, weaker whimpering; muffled voices, soothing it. A mosquito drones near my ear, but I am safe in my mosquito net. How I love a mosquito net! It is like a castle, impregnable to all. I can lie, stripped like a corpse, under my tented shroud, safe from all the bugs. Somewhere in the room a cricket starts up, the high pitch of its whine only really noticeable when, a little later, it stops. Later still I go for a pee. Outside, there is a thin, effervescent light. The compound is silent. The night is silent. I step like a thief across the pale sand.

We have a long morning of it at the *Centre*. As agreed, the seminar is to be completed this morning. As expected, there are not as many delegates today as there were yesterday. The night has seen a modest erosion: entirely, it must be said, on the male side. The first session is devoted to an exercise in which groups are asked to perform three tasks: to imagine what life will be like for them 10 years from now; to envisage how they would like it to be 10 years from now; and to think of what they might need to do differently over the next 10 years if they are to achieve what they want. This is a task requiring a sense of projection and aspiration that is less familiar to people who have such a strong belief in fate, for whom the uncertainties of tomorrow are largely left to the care of Allah – '*Insh'Allah*', 'God willing', is the standard phrase.

The groups have been selected carefully, though, each with a leader and someone who can write down the conclusions, and Ibrahim Tandia, Salif and Méline go around lending a hand. The conclusions are interesting. Whereas, on the one hand, most people are pessimistic about what they imagine the future holds for them – 'nothing will ever change here,' is the general attitude – they do not, on the other, have an alternative vision beyond the most simple improvements to their lives. They do not, or perhaps cannot, hold any great ambition. Ibrahim Tandia, by now confident in the trust of these people, ties up the morning session with a small lecture.

'Do you know what it is that holds you back?' he asks. 'Do you know what is your greatest threat? Is it the climate? Is it the poor markets? Is it politics? No. Your greatest threat is yourselves. You are strong people. I have seen that these last two days. You are able and courageous. You must believe you can change things for the better. You must believe in yourselves. You have your leaders. Some of you have already formed community groups and co-operatives. You have shown great skill and innovation with your farming techniques. Now is the time to be ambitious. Work with each other. Have a vision of your future and work towards it. I know you can do it. I have seen you, and I know how great you are,' he finishes, bringing to bear all the warmth and passion of his character.

Applause erupts. The women in their chairs to the right are standing, tears in their eyes; the odd person, such as the pastoralist with the wild hair who so stood out yesterday, is cheering, shouting comments back. It is a moment of unity and passion, even for the small 'White Moor' from yesterday – he who stormed out so ferociously – whom I'm now surprised to see tucked in amongst the crowd near the door. He might not be clapping, but he is here, his tantrum apparently forgotten by all.

That the seminar has been a success, we are sure. The next stage will be for Ibrahim Tandia to devise the principal elements of the community project Salif wishes to implement, one that will build on the momentum he has created and engage the communities in meaningful action to combat the many problems that face them. This is what we are hoping for and we are eager to hear what Ibrahim Tandia will propose.

Afternoon; and time to rest. Tomorrow, we are to be away all day, crossing the Senegal River into Senegal and visiting our Dohley Women's Market Garden project. It will be a long day, so we have set aside this afternoon for relaxing. Besides, Ibrahim Tandia needs to do some work, and we have planned a meeting of Salif's development group for the evening.

The sun is strong and mats are spread out in the shade under Mamadou's thatched lean-to in the compound. We lounge on cushions and thin mattresses. Tea is being made and the heat of the afternoon passes in idle chat and casual observation of the passing life of the compound. This is something that never tires me. I have always loved to lounge and watch the little troupes of naked toddlers staggering about as if drunk, by turns cajoled, bullied and cuddled by their elder siblings as they go on their journeys of discovery. Little girls, themselves not long out of toddlerhood, carry infants swaddled to their backs, pretending to be their mothers. Boys trundle around their ingenious trucks and cars constructed from old tin cans and bottle tops, complete with steering wheels and suspension as good as the real thing. Smaller ones might have a nice leaky battery to play with, or a plastic bag. Already you can see the characters emerging: those prone to being bullish; the nervy, bright ones; the bossy girls. Most of them are grubby to the extreme, the older ones dressed in long, stained T-shirts or, for the girls, ragged dresses. Most of the toddlers have green snot coming from their noses; clusters of flies gather at the corners of the smallest ones' eyes. Like children the world over, they squabble and fight, but always with a fierce eye for the adults, whose weight of approbation keeps them from going too far.

One time I saw a boy strike a girl. This brought him the most severe of condemnations and a thwacking from Mamadou that left him sobbing for many hours, to which no-one paid the slightest attention. Another time a boy was chased from the compound, shrieking with terror, escaping over a wall like a thief with shoes and stones thrown after him. I never did discover what he had done. The boys are treated toughly. They stick together in age-group gangs, roaming about warily, as at any moment they might be scolded or, worse, asked to perform a task. They are by no means cowed or dejected, though. Out of the compound, in the town, they have the bright, laughing eyes of mischief: '*Tubab, tubab,*' they will chant after me if they meet me down an alleyway – 'white man, white man'.

Twice a week such boys must visit the Qur'anic school, where for two hours they chant verses of the Qur'an. For the moment, they do not know the meaning of the Arabic words they have copied onto their wooden boards, but the better of them will learn; some, when they are older, might even memorize the entire book, at which time they might attain the title *Marabout*, or Holy One. The sound of their many voices chanting different verses at different pitches creates a melodious harmony that reverberates throughout the town.

The women are busy most of the afternoon and, when not busy, are certainly not idle. They may settle down together for a while on a mat, sipping tea and chatting, but their hands will be occupied, rubbing platters of millet flour into

couscous, picking over bowls of rice to remove tiny, teeth-wrecking stones, or fine-chopping haricot bean leaf. They will also spend many hours working on the intricate hair braids of their sisters or friends.

The women are remarkable always in their appearance. It is as if what life lacks in material and even cultural density – for the region is not of any great musical, artistic or ceremonial note – they make up for in their apparel. It is into clothes as opposed to anything else that the greatest effort is poured. And so the compound can seem at times like a catwalk. A young woman returning with a basin of water on her head is dressed in the most magnificent deep-purple, tie-dyed dress with laced white cuffs, gold gleaming at her ears, ranks of bracelets up her arms and skin oiled to a deep, honeyed brown. Another is lifting a large rock above her head – one that I would have difficulty wielding – and hurling it down onto a large piece of wood in order to break the wood into bits for the cooking fire, and despite the baseness of this lowest of all forms of wood-cutting technology, she is wearing a blue-and-pink checkered confection that would not look out of place in a fashion show. And, given only the thinnest provocation – the visit of an elderly aunt, say, or even just a trip to the market – the women will dress up in veritable ball gowns, their voluminous dresses quite startling in the dusty and dirty dilapidation of the town.

When there is a wedding or baptism, the magnificence of apparel is stunning. On such occasions, a compound will become a sea of mats and beauty. The men will also be resplendent in their brilliant white or sky-blue *bobos*, with gold-embroidered cuffs and collars. A sheep or even a cow will be slaughtered on such occasions. If it is a wedding, throughout the long afternoon people will spontaneously shout out their praise of the marrying couple. They will hold aloft a handful of cash, which will be given to the couple once their marriage has been officially completed on the payment of a dowry by the groom to the girl's father – often in the form of a cow or two – and after an Imam has blessed them; the bride will have been secluded for three weeks prior to this, unable to leave her family's house.

I sit and watch pretty Uma, the wife of Abou, Salif's younger brother, she with the hands of a blacksmith and eyes full of mirth. She is washing her children down, standing them in turn in a basin of water and soaping them up until they are white from head to toe. She squeezes snot from a toddler's nose and flicks it to the ground. She catches my eye as I watch her, and laughs.

There are a number of people about today and the comings and goings in the compound are frequent. A middle-aged cousin of Salif's from Dakar, the capital of Senegal, has shown up. I have met Barou N'Gam a number of times and have even visited him with Salif at his home in Dakar: a shanty in one of the most distant corners of that large city. He is an educated man with a neat black beard and a twinkle in his eyes. He is a pharmacist, but one without a job, as the pharmacy profession in Dakar, he tells me, is riddled with mafia-style cartelism from which he has been ousted. He is in Keniéba for two weeks only, 'on business'. He joins us on our mats under the thatch.

'Dakar is a nightmare now,' he tells me. 'They have dug up all the roads and it takes three hours to get from my house to the center of town.'

'You work in the center of town?' I ask, having forgotten how he earns a living now.

'No, no,' he says, 'there's no work in Senegal.'

'I thought Senegal was doing well,' I say.

'Ah,' he exclaims, 'the place is riddled with corruption. Everything... everything is corruption.' This surprises me, as I have long believed Senegal to be something of a beacon of hope in West Africa. But again, I think to myself, all is relative. What to an outsider may appear an acceptably functioning body politic and economy, to the man on the street who cannot get a job, who is hit for 'taxes' with every step he takes and who lives in a slum, it is a failed state. But I remember now how Barou N'Gam keeps soul and body together: he runs a small Qur'anic school in his house in Dakar and is a serial money borrower. This is probably why he is here now: to borrow money from Salif. He is a pleasant, friendly man, but, like so many, all too willing to rely on the family support network for his survival.

Another who appears this afternoon is a man I have seen before but remember now only when Salif introduces him to me as 'the old combatant'. He is an ex-soldier: a large, angular man dressed in a coarse farmer's tunic.

'You remember him,' Salif says, holding the man playfully by the arm before me as though he were an exhibit. 'He was a prisoner of Polisario in the north during the conflict over

Western Sahara. They kept him in a prison camp for five years.' The man grins cheerfully.

'Five years!' I exclaim, remembering now how very terrible I thought this captivity must have been in the remote wastes of the desert at the hands of a rebel group with probably barely enough resources to sustain itself, let alone prisoners. 'How were you captured?' I ask, Salif translating into Peul, as the ex-soldier cannot speak French.

'There was a battle in the desert,' Salif translates his reply, 'but as soon as the first shots were fired all our soldiers threw their guns down and surrendered. They were all conscripts, black men from the south, and they did not want to fight and be killed.'

The story has drawn people's attention and there is a good deal of hilarity at the part about the soldiers throwing their guns away and surrendering. The man is entirely unfazed, grinning broadly, even joining in the laughter.

'We were no match for Polisario,' he says. 'We did not know how to fight.'

'You certainly knew how to throw your rifles away,' Mariam, who is perched near us, adds. The man chuckles good-humoredly.

Alisanne, Amadou's brother back from France, is amongst us. He comes and sits next to me. This is the first chance we have had to chat, as he has been busy: '…paying visits,' he says a little wearily.

'You have to see everyone?'

'Most,' he says. 'As soon as I get back, all my relations come to see me, then I must visit each of their families and give them a little present.' He smiles.

'How much are you expected to give?'

He laughs at my inquisitiveness. 'There is no going rate. I give what I want: a thousand ouguiya… 5,000, the equivalent of two euros… 10 euros. Not much, but it adds up. These trips home are not cheap.'

For a number of years, Alisanne has been constructing a house on the outskirts of town, bringing money home with him for the next phase each time he returns. I have visited the house a number of times. It is a large, concrete-block building with a flat, cement-sealed roof. Airy and spacious inside, all floors and lower walls are tiled, and there is a bathroom, toilet and kitchen. Windows are barred and more or less permanently shuttered. All in all, the house represents a completely different manner of living to compound life. For a start, all is interior. There is no compound here around which different parts of the family can live. It is designed for a more nuclear group. The heat, glare and dust of the exterior world are cut out, as is the larger family. This is how the new generation wants to be. This is how Salif, I know, if he ever gets enough money together, wants to live.

'But what of the old people? What of the communal life? What of afternoons spent sitting on mats under a shady compound tree,' I have always wanted to ask, disappointed that this should be so. But the reality, I know, is that compound life is hard. The houses fall down with the rains; the children – at least according to Salif – run wild in unruly bands; hygiene is bad and everyone – again according to Salif – minds everyone else's business.

I have often wondered whether Alisanne will in fact ever return to Keniéba to live in his new house once it is finished; for this is clearly the main reason for building it. I ask him how the building is progressing.

'It's slow,' he says, 'but then so is everything here.'

'And when are you going to come back and live in this house?' I ask provocatively.

'Ah!' he exclaims with a grin. 'That only Allah knows.'

It will not be an easy move for him, that I know. And he has children now, who are French: will he abandon them?

It was two years ago that Alisanne visited me at my home

in Britain. For many years he had been on at me to come and see him in France, or for us at least to meet up somewhere. I had never seemed to manage it, and then one day he rang to say he was in England, staying with a friend in a large provincial town near to where I live. He was over to 'check out the employment opportunities', he told me.

He could not have been more charming and polite when he came to stay, instantly engaging my children's interest and affection. He did not remark on any particular aspect of the rural area in which I live or our life there. The only thing he found astonishing was the typical Sunday morning total absence of any signs of humanity in our small local town. Where on earth was everyone? We took him puffing up a mountain and fed him on roast lamb, which he thought 'a bit soft'. Then he went back to France, from where he rang a little later saying that he wanted to 'send' me his nine-year-old daughter. 'How do you mean?' I asked 'You want to bring her over?'

'Perhaps,' he said.

'How would I get her back to you?'

'You can keep her, until she's older,' he replied. I saw that I too was now a part of the 'network'. I declined, of course, which disconcerted Alisanne only slightly, but did not prevent him from insisting I send one of my daughters to him. 'She can stay with us a week… a month… as long as she wants, and she can learn French and see how Africans live,' he said.

Some years previously Salif had also come to stay with my family. Unlike Alisanne, he was overcome by the beauty of the countryside. It was May, and the countryside was indeed looking spectacular. 'Paradise,' was all he could whisper when asked one day what he made of the place. And the lush green fields and forests must indeed have seemed like some sort of agricultural heaven to one used to the wastes of Mauritania. I told him of the cold, black winters of rain; the lack of sunlight; the stresses of modern life. I did not want him to think it was paradise.

Late afternoon; and the light reflected on the wall across the compound grows a deeper shade of gold by the moment. Alisanne, Salif, Mamadou, Barou N'Gam, Abou, young Harouna making tea: we lounge, half asleep, sweaty, idly chatting. Ibrahim Tandia has been shut up in Salif's house all afternoon, working. Mustapha, our driver, and Harana, the vehicle 'boy', have been absent for the day, allowed to return to Kaédi until we next need them.

I watch the compound chickens. I have always found a certain amount of pathos in the activities of chickens. I have come to know these ones well, and their stories are often tragic: the brood of five chicks, one of which has a gammy leg and is always just a fraction too late for the grain of rice or crumb of food – day after day he weakens until his carcass ends up just a part of the compound litter; the not-so-dominant cockerel, bullied relentlessly by the preening 'king' rooster; the scrawny hen, next, you know, for the pot. I find the hens' attitudes to their chicks fascinating. They compete with them for food on an equal basis, shoving them aside and dashing for the crumbs, seeming to be entirely unaware of the maternal instinct. How they all survive is a mystery, as they are never fed, existing only on the most meagre of crumbs to be scratched from the barren compound floor. This does not prevent them, however, from having full social lives. Their relentless jealousies, courtships and couplings form a subliminal, background soap opera to that of the human compound.

The goats also draw my attention. During the day, only the kids are left behind in the compound. They are frisky, independent and eternally curious, constantly besieging kitchen areas and the mats from which people shoo them. They jump onto walls, balancing on their springy hooves before leaping off with an exuberance that is delightful to watch. They and their elders are such a different story from the droopy, silly sheep that plod about, apparently without a thought in their heads.

A ram is tied permanently to a post at the end of the compound. I find a strange fascination watching him repeat over and over again the full repertoire of his existence: circling the post, first one way, then the other, stopping still to bleat loudly at his surroundings; then scratching his nose with a hoof before continuing his eternal circling.

At one end of the compound is the stump of what was once a large, shady neem tree. The tree died some four or five years ago, and the fact that is has not been replaced is something that has nagged at me. What small effort, I have asked myself on many an occasion, would it take to plant a single tree that would benefit so many people? Compounds without trees are bare, glaring places. A tree creates shade, reduces the temperature and generally produces a vastly improved environment in which to live. And it is not just the failure to replace this tree that has perplexed me. Ever since I have been coming here I have been encouraging people to plant trees. Trees can do so much for an environment such as this. They bind soil, create humus and fodder from their leaves, break the wind, humidify the air, produce wood for construction and cooking. Nutritional and medicinal products can be had from their fruits and sap. Crops can be grown under them. And, most importantly, they are an investment in the future. They have the potential to rejuvenate this land. But never – or at least until very recently, as I hope to see tomorrow – have I persuaded a single person to plant a single tree. Even Salif, with the full advantage of the Mabafé family irrigation project, has never planted a single tree. Always there is a reason not to. Always it is next year.

One year, perhaps to satisfy my apparent need for trees, Salif took me to visit what he described as a 'forest', some 40 or so kilometers away. I was a little skeptical, having long been aware that the expression 'forest' generally meant little more than an area with slightly more scrub on it than usual. My shock, then, on Salif ushering me into a 50-hectare plantation of vast, mature trees was considerable. Here were mango trees a hundred foot in height, 50 years old. Eucalyptus, acacia, neem; exotic and native: thousands of trees were interspersed with fruit-tree plantations and even small vegetable plots. And so dense was the foliage, so all-encompassing the plantation, that the outside world – that Mauritania of dust and glare and desert – was completely excluded. This was the humid, green world of the tropics. I was astonished. How could this be? Here? Who had set it up?

The answer was that the plantation had been set up during the colonial era. It was now run by the Agricultural Research Department, the trees irrigated from the nearby Senegal River and overseen by a manager who, in the absence of any salary making it through to him, ran the place on a commercial basis, growing vegetables and selling the fruit from the trees. On closer inspection, as delightful as the place was, I could see that it was in poor condition and that many of the trees were in fact dying. But its existence illustrated to me a fundamental point: with a bit of water, a bit of investment and a bit of organizational ability, this apparently barren, desolate land could be transformed. So speaks the outsider! The question to ask is not simply whether the land can be transformed, but whether it can be transformed sustainably. Will the forest survive? If not, as seems likely, then this is not a path to development. It is an imposition rather than an evolution. As for the neem tree, that it will be replanted is fairly sure, but time is not measured in weeks or months or even years by some; it is measured in generations. When the time is ripe, it will grow once again.

The third and last of Harouna's teas has been taken and it is time for prayers. Salif rises and walks over to the water *bidon* to make his ablutions, washing hands, feet and face. Méline, Alisanne and Barou N'Gam follow suit, and soon they are all standing in a line facing east. Salif leads the prayers, raising his hands as he recites the opening prayers, then kneeling; then bowing three times to the earth. When they have finished, they remain seated on the ground for a while in quiet meditation. I watch them and I feel a twinge of envy. The day may be hot and long, life may be confusing and hard, but five times a day all becomes simple: you are nothing; you have nothing; everything, including your life, belongs to Allah. And in that, and in the routines of the five daily prayers, is a discipline that can only be beneficial in somewhere so very trying as the south of Mauritania.

It is time for a promenade. Salif suggests we pay a visit to the Keniéba Peace Corps volunteer.

The American Peace Corps is a phenomenon. Set up in the 1960s at the height of the Cold War, it was seen as a way of promoting US influence and creating understanding between Americans and others. Today, it has many thousands of volunteers who are sent with the minimum of support to some of the remotest villages in the world. Here, for two years, they do a little teaching or help with minor projects. Its personnel are young, generally well educated and middle class. I have come across them throughout Africa and without exception they have been friendly, idealistic and delighted in their postings. Life can be extremely tough for them, though, and they often suffer from illness and loneliness. They embed themselves deeply amongst the people with whom they are living, becoming a part of a family whose name they temporarily take. They have little contact with the outside world and are allowed home to see their families only once during the two years of their posting. I have always been fascinated by the almost filial relationship these Peace Corps Volunteers have with their hosts, as well as the paternalistic attitude their hosts take towards them.

Keniéba is on the Peace Corps map. It has had volunteers for many years and I can always be sure there is one around. We find Clare, or Aliou Demba, as is her local name, in the compound of a large family down a long passageway in a distant part of the town. We greet the inhabitants of the compound and they call for Aliou, who shortly appears from a hut. She is young – perhaps 22 – thin and pretty, wearing a typical African wrap-around dress, with a twist of material in her hair. She greets us formally, delicately shaking our hands and going through the full, traditional greeting repertoire of the locals, then asks whether we would prefer to talk in the compound or her hut. We decide on her hut and she leads us in, offering us cushions on her mat on the floor. I can see she is a little nervous, perhaps unsure of the purpose of our visit, perhaps just unused to seeing a fellow Westerner.

'Shall I make some tea?' she asks, then goes about gathering all the implements for a traditional tea. 'You've had the local tea. I've been learning to make it, but I'm still not very good at it,' she laughs. We chat and she tells us about her life here.

'I'm just coming up to the end of my first year,' she says, 'with one year to go. I think I am just now getting into it. At first, it was hard to understand what was going on, especially as my grasp of the language was so poor. I speak it more or less fluently now and am really starting to enjoy myself. These people are incredible,' she says, suddenly passionate. 'Binta, here,' and she indicates a young woman who was already in the hut when we came in and is sitting with us on the mat, 'can you believe that she is only 15 and was married last month.' She speaks some Peul to the girl who shakes her head embarrassedly. 'I asked if 15 was young to get married. They take on a lot of responsibility at such a young age,' she says. 'They are grown up by the time they are 15, often already with a child. Binta is from a village quite far from here and has come to live with her husband's family. It must be very hard for young girls like her. She comes to my room often and we are great friends now.' She leans over and, with a tenderness that is touching, takes Binta's hand in her own. 'We are friends, aren't we?' she says in English, smiling at the girl. 'I've been teaching her some English,' she explains. Binta dissolves into giggles.

I ask Clare how she finds compound life, aware as I am that it can be claustrophobic for a Westerner. Again, she laughs. 'Oh, it has its moments,' she says. 'The family like me to always eat with them, not anywhere else. They are very jealous of me, but we have an arrangement now that once a week I am allowed to eat with the local health nurse, with whom I do some work. That was a great concession on their part.'

There is something fresh and charming about Clare, although I can see she also has a steely determination. She has been ill, she tells us, and was for a long time quite lonely, but she has grown up considerably, she says, since she has been here. 'I will never forget my time in this village,' she remarks. 'It will stay with me always.' And I think how strange it is that soon the lives of Clare and her host family will part for ever, each to take on such different trajectories: she, no doubt, soon forgotten in the mill of everyday existence; they, always a distant and treasured memory, a souvenir of her young self. I ask Clare what she thinks her family will get from her stay and she looks at me curiously.

'I don't know,' she says, then laughs: 'Something, I hope.'

Dusk is already creeping over the town as we leave Clare's hut. We have arranged a meeting of Salif's development group. Arriving back at the compound, we find already congregated there the treasurer – a quiet, shy man who rarely speaks – and Demba Samba, Salif's main assistant. Demba Samba first reports on the problems they have been having trying to organize the many small-time farmers who want to hire the development group's tractor.

'There are too many of them,' he says in his forthright manner. 'They all want our tractor at the same time. They come to me all day; even in the middle of the night.' They have serviced nearly 22 different farmers groups this year, he tells us, representing some 300 farmers. 'It is very hard to co-ordinate,' he says.

Are we encouraging an unsustainable form of agriculture through the use of the development group's tractor for ploughing? That is the question I wish to look into. On the one hand, of course it is desirable that even small-scale African agriculture is increasingly incorporating more modern farming methods; on the other, though, much of the land being used in regions such as this is extremely marginal, with soils vulnerable to leaching from rain or displacement by wind. And, as always in remote places, there are problems with spare parts and maintenance, meaning tractors are not always reliable. Plus, the cost of fuel is so volatile that it amazes me that farmers and the tractor owners can find such an activity economical.

'The tractor must be expensive to hire,' I say. 'How can these farmers afford it? Surely, working their land by hand is more economical.'

'No. It is better for them to hire the tractor,' Demba Samba succinctly corrects me. 'A tractor can do in a couple of hours what by hand takes a week. And, because of the deepness of the plough, you get much better water penetration, leading to better crops and so better profits.'

'But surely the labor for hand work is free, done by family members,' I say.

'That is right,' Demba Samba replies. 'The weeding is done by family members either way, but there are not enough young men available nowadays for the first dig, as so many of them must go away on *aventure* to look for money. And to hire people in to do it is just not economical.'

I am still not clear about this but decide to drop it for

the moment. Ibrahim Tandia, who has been following our conversation, now joins in.

'People want to use tractors,' he says calmly, 'and rightly so. Agriculture in Africa must develop. But there are many different forms of development, each one suited to its own context. For example,' he goes on, 'there is much land being bought up in Africa at the moment for industrial farming: the so-called Land Grabs. Many see this as the way forward for African agriculture: farming on a large scale, with the most modern methods producing the largest yields. And in some circumstances this might indeed be sustainable. But even when it is, these big projects, as some of us know only too well, are not as easy to operate as many seem to think. They rely on stable governments, stable market prices and a stable climate, none of which are currently very available. And of course the fact is that the people whose lands are used for these schemes – the local people – are often those who fare worst, meaning that the very people improved agriculture should be helping – the poor – are in fact those who benefit the least.' Ibrahim Tandia pauses.

'But there is another way forward,' he says, 'one that favors local people.' This is what we have been waiting for: his take on the situation; his proposal.

'It is a way,' he goes on, 'that local people are in many respects already implementing, if not very efficiently; a way that is particularly suited to this region, which is very underdeveloped.'

Development, Ibrahim Tandia tells us, especially in regions like this, is not just about food or health or housing issues. It is about empowerment – empowering people to be able to make their own choices. It is about using what is available locally and about building up some resilience to the uncertainties of the volatile world that surrounds us. This means, he says, listening to people: hearing their concerns and ideas. And it means, most importantly, letting local people claim ownership of the available resources, whether these be land, water or even the availability of labor. And the best way of doing this is for local people to use those resources effectively, and to unite themselves into viable economic forces that can stand up to the outside interests that wish to take over their land.

'What we are talking about,' he says, 'is simply improved farming methods, better organization and, most importantly – and this is what I tried to impress on people this morning in my closing speech at the seminar – confidence. Farming methods must be better adapted to current market and climatic circumstances; people must learn to co-operate with one another and organize themselves into effective groupings; and they must have the confidence to step out of old ways, believe in and make the most of themselves.'

'What we will have then,' he says, a gleam now discernible in his eye, 'is a project that incorporates all of these. There will be many elements: integration of livestock with agriculture; organizational and management training; rice intensification and diversification; an animal health program; instruction in new planting methods, in rain-catchment, in compost making. These and other activities will be conducted in different locations with farmers across all the various agricultural sectors. Other farmers will come to see them with their own eyes. Seeing Is Believing. That will be our motto. The project will be of five years' duration, with learning seminars at mid- and end-point, and during its course much will be learnt about unity and co-operation.'

'Much of this,' he finishes, 'is of course what you and the farmers have in some ways been doing for a long time already. But I hope I can add a little impetus and a little structure to your work.'

We are amateurs, Salif and I. It is a pleasure to hear someone as experienced as Ibrahim Tandia.

Demba Samba speaks up. 'It's good,' he says.'Very good.

But how are we going to do it?'

'Through hard work, of course,' Ibrahim Tandia laughs. 'Plus the project plan I will provide you with.'

As I climb under my mosquito net that night I feel a confidence I have not had for a while: we did the right thing in bringing Ibrahim Tandia here.

8 Across the Senegal River

The socialist survivor... Does foreign aid undermine self-help?... The monster pump... Why large, centralized schemes fail... Crossing the river by dugout... The women's co-op and their organic bounty... A grand gift... Africans in America

Mustapha, our driver, and Harana, the vehicle 'boy', are back with the Toyota. They are waiting for us first thing in the morning. We are going to visit our Dohley Women's Market Garden Project just over the Senegal River: nine hectares of vegetables farmed by the 312 members of the Dohley Women's Co-operative. We will travel there via Kaédi in order to pick up Monsieur Po, the project agronomist and manager. We will not be crossing into Senegal at the official border post there, however, slipping instead quietly and bureaucracy-free by dugout canoe across the Senegal River further upstream.

We cruise with disorientating ease back up the *piste* to Kaédi in the Toyota. Monsieur Po we find in his house in a suburb of town that looks as though it has been struck by an earthquake: low, brown buildings are everywhere tumbled down, their earthen bricks dissolving back into the brown earth from which they came. Children and families with washing lines and goats inhabit parts of compounds still in use, and here and there the odd fully functioning homestead with shiny tin roofs and a large satellite dish survives. It is in one of these that we find Monsieur Po.

Monsieur Po appeared on the scene some years ago: a small, wiry man with a sharp look in his eyes. I did not take to him at first. He was wearing a 'Mao' safari suit – a buttoned-up, collarless garment in utilitarian blue – and seemed fastidious and a little irritable. He was an administrator in a near-defunct government agricultural research agency and I thought him one of those types devoted to efficiency and the detail of procedure: the sort whose kingdom the world over is the minutiae of bureaucracy. But Monsieur Po grew on me and in time I came to see that his creed was not authoritarianism but socialism. He sprang from that now-extinct period when a number of African countries experimented with Marxism, promoting nationhood over tribalism, even going to the lengths in some places of moving people off their lands and forming soviet-style farm collectives. It was not successful. Economies collapsed, undermined by inefficiency, politics and corruption; riots and coups d'état ensued. But it did breed many educated, idealistic young people for whom the post-independence belief that Black Africa could be reborn on the back of hard work and diligence still rang true.

Some years ago there were still many of these people around. I used to come across them on my travels: teachers in far-distant villages sticking diligently to their curriculum despite the fact that they had not been paid for a year-and-a-half and must take their classes under a tree; or administrators in government departments that had been stripped by their directors of all resources but continued to do the best they could in the circumstances: people who believed in the possibility of a modern Black Africa where nationhood was greater than tribehood and Africans had as much ability as anyone else. Monsieur Po is a remnant of such people and we have been lucky to get our hands on him, as he is a man of both commitment and ability.

'Monsieur Peter, Salif,' he greets us in his compound, eyes bright. Ibrahim Tandia has gone off on an errand in the Toyota. There are a number of people about: wife – wives? – offspring, others; we greet them only briefly as Monsieur Po has never made any effort to introduce his family to us. In a corner of the compound sits the shell of a car against which is leant the small motorbike we have provided Monsieur Po with. We go into his room in one of the buildings surrounding the compound, which is overflowing with files and paperwork. In the corner is a television set with a cloth draped over it, and an open laptop lies in the middle of the carpeted floor.

'You will take some tea and eat?' Monsieur Po asks, then barks an order out the door. We exchange a few pleasantries but before long we are delving into the paperwork side of the project.

The Dohley Women's Market Garden Project is in the third of its four funded years and, so far, it has been a success, inspiring people over a large region and even featuring on local radio. This is mainly due to the hard work of the members of the Dohley Women's Co-operative, but is also in no small part a result of the meticulous care employed during the planning phase.

It was some five years ago that the President of the Co-operative, one Madame Diop, approached Salif, asking him whether his development group could help them resurrect their currently defunct market-gardening activities. They had a large nine-hectare site near to the Senegal River but no way of irrigating it. Previously they had had a pump, but this had grown old and had broken down, and they did not have the money to replace it. Madame Diop, the President, produced a formal dossier of request.

From the start the project looked as though it had potential, although there were a few issues that I felt needed sorting out before we made any commitment. The primary of these revolved around the number of newly built, modern houses I had noticed on my first visit, which surrounded the otherwise impoverished traditional center of the village. These new houses were clearly the property of expatriates, those from the area now living in the cities of West Africa or elsewhere. One of them, I noticed, even had a Mercedes parked outside its door. There was money here. What on earth, then, were these people doing asking Salif and me for funds? They should be raising them from within their own community. I asked Salif about this. I asked Monsieur Po. I asked Madame Diop. But it took some considerable time before I got an answer I could understand.

The issue seemed important to me, as it brought into focus a fundamental question: were foreign development agencies deemed a 'soft touch' and, as such, no matter how good their intentions, undermining the more natural dynamic of self-help?

There was money around: indeed, there is generally money around when there are investment opportunities. Banks lend money, entrepreneurs invest it; it can be winkled out of family members. But this money is only readily available if the investment opportunity is indeed genuine. No-one is happy about producing funds for schemes that have little chance of giving a return. And so it is quite possible to have a community where some members – probably non-resident ones – have some money while the rest exist in a state of poverty. Those with funds will certainly fulfil their duty and send money home, money that will fend off total destitution – and even this amount, as any expatriate will tell you, tends to be considerable – but they will be reluctant to go beyond this and invest, for example, in local agricultural enterprises if they see that the local economy is dysfunctional. They know only too well where that will end; there are certainly plenty of examples in the irrigation sector, on some of which they may have already burnt their fingers. It is better to spend any hard-earned, surplus money in the solid bricks and mortar of a building than to throw it away on some hopeless business venture. The result of this is that people and regions can slip further and further into poverty despite the fact that, in theory at least, money is available. What was needed here, then, it seemed clear, was the development of a farming model that, even in the difficult local context, could be seen to turn a genuine profit, one that would encourage local investment. We would work with the Dohley Women's Co-operative and try to develop with them such a model; we would inspire local people to invest in it; and we would use the results of the project as an example to others. It would not be rocket science, but would be based on the simple business principle of keeping input costs down while increasing outputs like yields and produce value.

The plan Monsieur Po and the members of the Dohley Women's Co-operative came up with was based on the use of a small diesel pump drawing water from the Senegal River involving a large, camel-proof fence, bands of windbreak, forestry and fruit trees, a piped water distribution system and organic farming practices that reduced input costs while increasing yields. A hierarchy of responsibility was devised, with the highly capable and quietly indomitable Madame Diop at the top, and co-operative financial management was put on a more sustainable basis, with stipends due strictly on a monthly basis, and reinvestment in the scheme compulsory.

From the start, the enthusiasm with which the women conducted the project was remarkable and, within only a few weeks of our commitment to it, 300 compost piles had been created. Now, only four years on, the full nine hectares are being exploited, each of the 312 women having a minimum of two *planches* of land, each *planche* measuring 200 square meters. Water management and use is so efficient that the entire scheme is capable of being irrigated by the

comparatively tiny one-cylinder water pump stationed at the Senegal River a few hundred meters away. And, because of the high compost use and the water retention qualities it gives to the soil, growing periods are extended, meaning that each year the women can squeeze in three successive vegetable seasons, the produce of which, again because of the compost, always finds a ready market as it looks, tastes and conserves better. At the last project evaluation, local families reported incomes up by 30 per cent. Not that there haven't been 'issues' along the way, one of which crops up as Monsieur Po and I now go through the year's project reports on the floor of his room.

'Yes, the expatriates have fully paid for the second pump and it was delivered in the middle of the year,' Monsieur Po says, referring to the project element that required the local people to pay for a standby pump. 'In fact,' he goes on, 'it has already proved useful as the one-cylinder pump was out of action for some weeks, having been submerged in the rising waters of the river. It is mounted on a floating platform,' he continues, 'which will protect it from the river and also make it easier to maneuver, as, being a three-cylinder pump, it is very heavy.'

'Did you say three cylinders?' I ask.

'Yes, it's a three-cylinder pump,' Monsieur Po repeats.

This is a massive pump and alarm bells are ringing in my head. One of the main purposes of the project is to minimize water usage and so reduce costs, not something likely to be achieved by a pump that can produce up to 10 times the volume of water of our small pump.

'Why have they bought such a large pump?' I ask.

'They got it for a good price,' Monsieur Po says. 'It is some years old.'

I am not happy. No longer can we demonstrate, it seems to me, that nine hectares can be irrigated with a small capacity of water. Even the flood-irrigation people don't have three cylinder pumps.

'It's too big,' I say. 'Surely, it will be impossible for the Co-operative now to restrict its water usage, and their diesel costs are going to go right up.'

Monsieur Po considers for a moment. 'It's true,' he says, 'it is too large, but that's what they bought: what can we do?'

'It won't change anything,' Salif adds. 'It's only the standby pump. They won't use it all the time.'

'The temptation will always be there,' I say. 'One flick of the switch and they can have their entire week's worth of water in a day.'

'They won't do that,' Salif replies. 'The water channels couldn't take it for long, anyway.'

I've noticed in the Co-operative's annual finances, which are open in front of us, that a not-inconsequential sum of money has been used this year to purchase a quantity of the 25-centimeter piping needed for large pumps. 'They've invested in large-diameter piping, I see,' I say. 'Presumably that's to use with the pump.'

'Yes, that's right,' Salif replies.

'Then it seems to me they intend on using the large pump at least to some significant degree,' I say.

'No, not necessarily,' Salif replies with a certain finality in his voice. I am still not happy.

'I think you don't need to worry yourself too much,' Monsieur Po intervenes. 'It won't change a thing.' I decide to drop the subject. When we get to Dohley, things might look different, as they so often do.

There are a number of other more minor points that need ironing out about the project, but on the whole I can see that things are going well, and I am keen to get out there and see it all with my own eyes.

'Do the women know we are coming?' I ask tentatively, as I prefer to arrive in Dohley unannounced. The 312 women of the Co-operative, as well as probably double that number in younger sisters and other female non-members, have a tendency to use any excuse for a party, and my and Salif's arrival can sometimes descend into a mêlée of such intensity that clear thinking, or indeed mental survival at all, is nearly impossible. Salif smiles. 'They don't know which day we are coming,' he says, 'but they know you are here and that we are coming this week.'

Monsieur Po laughs. 'They've got something planned, I can tell you that. You're not going to get away with a quiet visit this time.'

Later Ibrahim Tandia appears with Mustapha and Harana in the Toyota. Although it is still barely midday, a cloth is spread on Monsieur Po's floor and a meal of rice and fish produced. Mustapha is a changed man here in Kaédi. Gone is his shyness. Although perhaps not yet what could be called forthcoming, he digs into the food with relish, scooping up

vast quantities in his large hand, and sits back afterwards with a contented look on his face. Harana, younger and more cheerful by disposition, laughs at my messy eating technique.

'Here, like this,' he says using his few words of French and showing me how to squeeze the rice into a neat, mouth-sized ball.

Our meal finished, we set off for Dohley, crossing the top of a small dam where the Moshe joins its larger brother, the Senegal River.

The Senegal River, which here acts as the border between Mauritania and Senegal, is a slowly surging body of sandy-colored water around 600 meters wide. In the dry season, flat 'beach' areas, where patches of maize are grown and the odd dugout is pulled up, hem its length. There is no great profusion of vegetation hugging its banks; instead, it passes nakedly through the parched savannahs of the Sahel like the great drainage ditch it really is. It traverses sparsely populated lands and only a few fisherfolk ply its waters. Villages are rare on its banks. This is because in the rainy season the river transforms itself. From being a brown, sleepy snake, it becomes with frightening speed an uncontrollable

monster. It will rise seven or eight meters in a day, flooding many millions of hectares of river valley until there is a vast glinting inland sea stretching from horizon to horizon.

Many fisherfolk stand down by the water's edge where we cross the dam, poised like herons, ready to spin their nets out over the churning patch where the Moshe and Senegal rivers merge. Here, we find a police post. This is a border area, and so a certain tension prevails, especially since the Islamist troubles in neighboring Mali.

'Where are you going?' demands the police officer who walks over to us after snapping us a smart salute. We tell him we are going up country to visit a village. He eyes us suspiciously. Salif has reported the same by phone to the adjutant.

'Papers,' he says.

We hand him our various IDs and he takes them off into his hut. Time passes. Might we be prohibited from proceeding? Shortly, he is back.

'Have a good day,' he says, handing our papers back through the vehicle window. I feel guilty. It is a little naughty of me, I know, to be crossing the border in this way. But then Dohley is so easily accessible from where we are going to cross, directly on the opposite bank; we will be there only a few hours; and crossing at the official post in Kaédi might not only be problematic as the status of the border's openness is not always clear, but it would also leave us in quite the wrong place without any transport. Emphatically, I'm afraid, this is far easier.

We skirt a large area of rice paddies. This is one of the huge, government-run irrigation schemes that were set up at the same time as the dams were built on the Moshe and Senegal rivers, altering the hydrology of the region. It is surrounded by a tall bund protecting it from floods and covers some 2,000 hectares. A few peasants with straw hats work in the plots they hire from the centrally managed scheme in exchange for a percentage of their harvests. Canals of water dissect the plain, with sluices and ditches servicing different areas. It looks impressive, but Salif is dismissive of it. For him, it demonstrates exactly why it is that large, centrally managed schemes do not work.

'The directors treat the scheme as a source of private income,' he says. 'The yields here are some of the lowest in the region. Water supply is inconsistent and the soils have become salty.' People, he says, are charged such a high price for the inputs that it is very hard for them to make any profit and much of the land is in fact left uncultivated.

We traverse after this a wild, scrubby country a little inland from the river. This is a route Monsieur Po knows only too well, as three days every month he must take it to visit Dohley.

'You should have seen it last year,' he says. 'I could only come on bicycle as there were floods everywhere. Even then I had to wade through areas of water carrying my bike.' I try to imagine Monsieur Po in such a posture, but somehow cannot.

In one place we pass the remains of a village. This is a poignant spot that draws disapproving clicks of the tongue from those in the vehicle, for this is one of the many villages whose inhabitants were thrown over the border during the period of ethnic troubles in the country. A few broken huts stand about on the bare earth; the shards of a shattered water jar; the stump of a tree.

Finally we ease our way over broken ground towards a tall tree that turns out to be at the top of the bank overlooking the Senegal River. Far on the other side can be seen a straggle of low, brown buildings: Dohley.

The pirogue owner paddles slowly across the river, working diagonally upstream against the current in order to keep us on target. Halfway across, Ibrahim Tandia grabs a spare paddle in the bottom of the boat and rolls up his sleeves to lend a hand.

'This is the life!' he shouts, his face lit and happy, making us all laugh. As soon as we reach Dohley he will leave us, starting his long journey back through Senegal to Dakar, then on to Europe. Having Ibrahim Tandia with us has been a privilege and an inspiration. Both Salif and I have learned much from him. It certainly seems like he has enjoyed his trip.

By the time we reach the far side, a crowd has gathered: as Monsieur Po predicted, we are not going to get away with a quiet visit this time. An uproar of welcome ensues as soon

as we step ashore and hands in the dozens are thrust at us to shake. Women are singing and doing little impromptu dances, ululating. Children whirl around like tops. We are propelled with the throng up the slope and towards a large, thatched communal area. Here Madame Diop, the Co-operative President, and members of the management committee are waiting to meet us.

Madame Diop is a woman of deceptive qualities. She has eyes full of compassion and a quiet, even shy, manner, but she also has a tangible strength and is well respected. She ushers us over to where a large spread of mats has been prepared. Here we are regally sat down. Not all the 312 members of the Co-operative are present, but by the looks of things a great many of them are, seated now in all their finery in a great press around us: noisy, unruly and laughing with a certain mischievousness in their eyes. I do not feel comfortable but I know only good will is intended. The women want to make known their great appreciation for being given the chance to create the irrigation scheme. They want to impress on Salif, Monsieur Po and me their gratitude. We have little choice in the matter.

Madame Diop sits beside us, as do a couple of women from the management committee whom I know well: one, a woman carrying the young infant she has had since I last saw her, has the dark, flashing eyes of an Amazon; the other is fair, pretty and sophisticated-looking. Both speak French, which is unusual among village women, and indicates probably that they are not Dohley-born but have ended up here through marriage, perhaps from the capital or some other large town.

'How has the year been?' I half shout to them amid the noise.

'Aiee,' the one with the flashing eyes replies, 'you should have seen the floods. They came right up to here where we are sitting. It was very frightening.'

The other smiles with astonishing gentleness. 'We've had a

good year,' she says softly. 'The project has given us much to do, and for this we are happy.'

A group of men appear and step their way self-consciously through the crowd to shake our hands. The menfolk of Dohley are as proud of the irrigation scheme as the women. They are proud of the part they have played in it, for it was their physical labor that constructed the fence and did much of the initial groundwork. And they are proud of what the women have achieved. Time and again I have heard this repeated: how proud the menfolk are of what the women have achieved. Here, at least, the conflict between the sexes that so occupies much of the development world is not so apparent.

The men, having shaken our hands, look about for places on the mats. Madame Diop is one of the first to stand up and accommodate them, as space is at a premium. This is done with graciousness, though, and the men are appreciative. Any deference implied, one can clearly see, is purely formal.

Soon another group of men can be seen approaching the back of the crowd. These are the old men, the village elders, and Salif quickly rises to go over and greet them. I too rise and put my shoes back on to go over and shake their hands. Once this is completed, Salif and I retake our places, and Madame Diop stands to make a short speech, Salif translating, as she does not speak French. We are thanked for coming, Allah is thanked for bringing us here and various other themes along similar lines are introduced, but I can see that Madame Diop is at pains to restrict herself, as the main event, I am aware, is reserved for later in the afternoon. There is some clapping from the assembled women when she finishes and an elderly lady also rises to give a speech, which, when it appears to be taking on too much momentum, Madame Diop politely interrupts, explaining that the plan is for us to visit the co-operative fields before it gets too late. A group of 10 or 15 of us now extract ourselves from the crowd – Monsieur Po, Salif and I; Madame Diop and a number of other women;

and a couple of the men – and we make our way out into the brilliant white glare of the mid-afternoon.

The co-operative fields are a kilometer outside the village over a naked plain. They stand only some 200 meters from the bank of the Senegal River, surrounded by a tall wire-mesh fence. When the project first started, the nine hectares consisted of the same baked plain that surrounds them: an expanse of apparently barren desert, as hard and bald as concrete. Now, only three years into development, the land is transformed. Along one side stands a windbreak of eucalyptus trees, along the near side of which runs a 10-meter strip of forestry, consisting of species that have medicinal or other benefits such as gum Arabic, neem and acacia. At one end of the scheme is a small banana plantation and an area planted with mango and citrus trees in between whose rows, and in the shade of which, certain crops are grown. The rest of the land is divided up into two separate sets of plots that the women work individually.

The nearer of the two sets was the first to be developed and has already produced three harvests; the further one is just now coming into development. Pipes run from the irrigation pump down by the river up into the scheme from where open channels take the water to the plots. One large water basin and a number of smaller ones are dotted about. These are unused and will probably remain so, as the initial plan for women to draw water by bucket from the smaller basins did not work out. For a start, there was not enough water pressure to carry sufficient water from the larger tank to the smaller ones. Then it was found that the women who appeared earliest in the day to irrigate their plots quickly used up what water there was, leaving none for those who came later.

Indeed, there have been many 'evolutions' during the course of the project. For example, it was found that many of the women were less than conscientious when it came to caring for those parts of the scheme that were owned collectively, with profits paid into the Co-operative's exchequer, as opposed to those from which the profits were kept individually. These first included all the trees, as well as certain crops, and poor attention to irrigation schedules had resulted in considerable losses. This led to a change to the Co-operative constitution allowing for fines to be brought against any such culprits. In another example, initially one small area of the scheme was to employ drip irrigation, a system that uses only the bare minimum of water, but it was decided that this should be dropped as it required a level of management the women might be unable to maintain. There have been many other changes during the course of the project, some of which have cost money, some of which haven't. But from the start, the objective was for the project to evolve, experiment and discover, and if this was to lead to some losses, so be it.

It is satisfying to see the land green and in production; to hear the enthusiasm of the women; and to know that people travel from far and wide to come and see the 'marvel' of the Dohley Women's Market Garden. This local fame of the project, I am aware, is not so much to do with any successes it might have achieved – although certainly people are also interested in these – as to do with the fact that it has happened at all. Such is the cynicism directed at development projects in the region that people were astonished to see something beyond words and rhetoric actually manifest itself.

We make our way across the plain towards the co-operative fields. A tall, lugubrious man with a goatee beard keeps pace with me. This is Abou Mody, leader of the village youth league and self-appointed village 'overseer' of the women's market garden scheme. It was the young men of the village, under this older man's supervision, who constructed the fence and did much of the initial land and canal work for the scheme, and of this Abou Mody is immensely proud. He

maintains a proprietorial interest in the project.

'We were very lucky this year,' he announces as we walk. 'Even though the floods were exceptional, they did not reach the scheme.'

'Are the co-operative lands ever flooded?' I ask. 'They are very close to the river.'

'Never – they're on high ground and never flood… never,' he adds with an emphasis that is then undermined by his next statement: 'They only flooded a little this year.'

Monsieur Po, who is walking beside us, intervenes: 'The water caught just one corner of the land, but nothing was lost. One minute there is no water in this land,' he adds, 'and the next you are up to your neck in it.'

We come to the large metal signboard announcing in proud, spidery writing the details of the market garden: who funded it, who owns it and how many hectares it covers. I take a photograph of Monsieur Po and Salif standing beside it.

Down by the river we find the water pump, or rather

pumps. The small one-cylinder one we have provided, which has been shown to be capable of irrigating the full nine hectares despite its small size, is on one side, currently unused. In the water on a floating metal platform sits the huge three-cylinder pump the community bought as a standby. It is connected to a system of large pipes running up and over the bank towards the scheme. We follow the pipes and spend the next half hour wandering about the market-garden fields. It is the end of the cool, dry season, the main vegetable-growing period, and everywhere the women's plots are in production. Cabbages, carrots, onions, tomatoes, lettuce, mint, sweet potatoes, turnip and marrow: the list of varieties is long and in places there are even some crops left over from the previous hot season, such as hibiscus, aubergine, chili and manioc. These, Monsieur Po tells me, should not be here, as they are by now yielding very little and are taking up valuable space that should have been planted with the cool-season vegetables.

'But I cannot get the women to uproot crops that are still in production, no matter how poor that production,' he says. 'They do not like doing it and fail to understand the importance of respecting the correct seasons. The result is that many of them are only getting one or two seasons on much of their land, when they could be getting three. This affects the profitability of the whole scheme.'

The women who have accompanied us to the fields, and the few who are already there, are unconcerned with such quibbles, however. They delight in showing me their crops and produce and soon set up a great merriment of dancing and singing. When I take my camera out for some photographs, they pose magnificently, insisting that Monsieur Po, for whom they clearly have an affection, join them.

We do not linger long at the scheme as the afternoon heat is like a sledgehammer, battering the tops of our heads, and there is still much to be got through back in the village.

Once we have inspected the forestry and fruit trees and walked along the windbreak – I am astonished to see that the eucalyptuses have now grown six meters since they were planted as seedlings three years ago – we make our way back.

We are installed on the balcony of Madame Diop's house. This is next to the central thatched area where the majority of the women are still gathered. Here we are served a meal of rice and fish with plenty of vegetables followed by a Lipton's tea for me, the production of which becomes something of a performance as the entire village needs to be scoured before the requisite glass and teaspoon can be found. Once all is accomplished, and Salif, Monsieur Po and myself are relaxed and comfortable on our cushions on our mat at the end of the balcony, the Co-operative's committee members gather before us for a meeting.

The whole scene strikes me as somewhat unfortunate: the men positioned regally on their 'dais'; the women deferential and subjugated before them. It is not how it should be; not that anyone else has a problem with this, and the meeting goes ahead with full, non-deferential participation. The issues of the pump, the lack of crop rotation and a problem concerning management of the irrigation system – which the women seem disinclined to take responsibility for – are thoroughly discussed with the following conclusions: the large three-cylinder pump – which the women insist they dislike using anyway because it is very hard to get going and uses up so much fuel – will be taken off its floating platform and replaced with the smaller pump until a new platform can be bought for that, thereby re-establishing the primary project objective of showing that high input costs are not required to run such schemes; the crop-rotation issue will be sorted out by dedicating a certain area

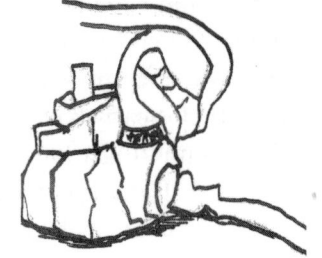

to the use of only the hot-season vegetables – meaning the women's natural abhorrence for cutting still-yielding plants can be accommodated, as the crops can remain there all year if necessary; and the issue concerning the women's disinclination to manage the water-distribution system will be resolved by the simple expedient of hiring a man to do the job. Minutiae these may all be, but they are important issues for which intelligent, pragmatic solutions are ably delivered.

Speech making: we are gathered outside, back on the mats. The crowd has swelled and there is a certain tension, or sense of anticipation, that I cannot quite fathom. Salif, Monsieur Po and I face the crowd, with Madame Diop and various committee members to our left. Abou Mody and a couple of other men stand nearby. The speech making goes on for a long time. Salif begins briefly enough, thanking all for their participation in the project and outlining its accomplishments. I am then asked to say a few words and I make efforts to produce a speech that at least half lives up to the expectations of people for whom the oral tradition is something of an art form.

Then Madame Diop rises and demonstrates a full and elaborate example of that art. Salif attempts interpretation, although I can tell by the brevity of his statements that much of what Madame Diop is saying goes untranslated. This does not matter. Nor does it matter that the speech seems to take on a circular structure, coming back periodically to where it began. What comes across is passion, humility, gratitude and courage. Madame Diop stabs the air to make her points; draws to long, poignant pauses. She speaks softly, at times almost inaudibly; then her voice rises: loud, strong and full of determination. Salif, Monsieur Po and I come in for much praise, as do the co-operative women who also, though, undergo a period of significant finger wagging. Allah features largely. The women listen, clap and murmur agreement. Each time Madame Diop draws to a pause, I think: 'surely now she has finished'. But each time she sets off once more. Her voice becomes all: mesmeric, enrapturing. We all sway and murmur to its rhythms. Then suddenly, almost before I am aware of it, she has stopped and another has taken her place.

A series of speakers now take the floor, ending with the old woman who had been interrupted earlier on, before we went to the fields. She is a tall woman wrapped in a sky-blue shawl, with a face as smoothly wrinkled as a prune. She speaks for a long time, sometimes to the apparent hilarity of her audience. She speaks of many things, some quite unconnected to the project, and, as she does so, it occurs to me how very democratic is the oral tradition. Each can have his or her say, no matter how apparently irrelevant the content.

It is evening now and the light is soft, and suddenly there is a shift in the atmosphere. A small commotion takes place at the back of the crowd; then someone is making their way towards the front carrying a package. A buzz of excitement fills the air and I am aware that everyone is looking at me. I click. There's to be a presentation. This is what the sense of anticipation was about. The person arrives at the front and hands the package to Madame Diop, who, in turn, passes it on to me, grinning hugely. In my hands is a parcel – a present – wrapped in gold, shiny wrapping paper. I am amazed. Never before in rural Africa have I come across the concept of wrapping paper and wrapped presents. This is like a Christmas gift. I know only too well the amount of thought and effort that must have gone into its production. Everyone is waiting.

'Open it,' Monsieur Po says. 'It is their present for you.'

I cannot tear the paper off as I would at home as it seems here a criminal waste, so I carefully part the sticky tape with which it is held together and reveal a set of magnificent traditional men's clothes: a beautiful sky blue *bobo* hemmed with gold stitching and starched to an immaculate crispness;

and a pair of short, baggy trousers of the same material. I have no choice, of course. I must put the *bobo* on, and, as I pull it over my head, the whole crowd bursts into uproarious laughter. I am moved.

As if this were a signal, suddenly now the formal part of the evening is over. The crowd rises and erupts. Singing, dancing, shouting and laughing, the women and huge quantities of near-hysterical children and youths create a great mêlée of commotion. Amidst this, a smart-looking youngish lady with a round, friendly face suddenly appears beside me and delicately offers me her hand to shake. She introduces herself and tells me she is from Dohley but lives in Paris, from where she has just today arrived. She wants me to know how very appreciative she and all the women of Dohley are of the market garden: how very proud of it they are. She is earnest and sincere, and I find these words from someone having so recently come from the comparative opulence of western Europe highly moving. Her words remind me that it is not so much the financial input we have provided that is important – as presumably this would not so impress someone from Paris – but the motivational and organizational contributions that have made such a difference.

Next, two men appear whom I have also not seen before.

'Howdyado,' one of them reels out in English spoken in a strong American accent. 'How d'ya like it here?' I am a little taken aback.

'Hi,' I stutter, in English. 'Where are you from?'

'Louisiana,' is the reply.

For some reason I have the urge to laugh. Here I am, wearing a sky-blue *bobo*, standing in a throng of 300 over-excited people in the pink evening light, exhausted, dirty and a little dizzy, and someone is speaking to me in the broad drawl of the American south.

'What are you doing here?' I ask, half shouting because of the noise. A child falls against me. A woman is clapping by my ear.

'We're back for a holiday. This is our home,' the man shouts back. 'We work in Louisiana.'

'How is it in Louisiana?' I ask, unable to think of anything else to say.

'It's okay,' is the simple response. An idea occurs to me.

'And when you're there,' I shout, 'do you live as Africans or Americans?' It's a strange question, I know, and I ask it half jestingly, but then, because I am actually quite interested in the response, I add: 'For example, do you eat African food from a single platter, like here, or use a knife and fork?'

The man is unfazed. 'We live as Africans. Of course,' he says.

Our conversation does not proceed beyond this point, because at this moment Monsieur Po appears and tells me it is time to go: we are to make our way down to the river's edge where a pirogue is waiting to take us back to Mauritania. I have just time to shake the hands of the two 'Americans', and then we are off, the crowd following close behind.

Down at the water's edge, the splendor of deep evening is in full swing: the river, a strip of mercury; the sky, hemmed in mauve. The women are surpassing themselves and the uproar is all-encompassing. I struggle through to where the pirogue is pulled up in the water and leap onto its pointed prow. Monsieur Po and Salif clamber in behind me. Hands are thrust at us to shake: Madame Diop, Abou Mody, members of the committee, giggling boys, many women. And then the boat is pushing out into the current. There are shouts and cries of farewell as we paddle slowly away from the shore. Slowly, gradually, the din recedes.

For a long time we can see and hear the crowd still laughing and singing on the shore, but soon it is the peace and smooth ripple of the river that holds us in its grasp. Now I can see how near night it is: Dohley disintegrating into the darkness of the shore, the sky mostly black. We are silent as we pass the halfway mark, inhaling the clear, musky moistness of the river, only the slurp and gurgle of the paddle audible as it churns rhythmically at the dark water. On the far bank, on the Mauritanian side, I can see the silhouette of the Toyota beside the tree. When we reach the shore, we come to a halt with a lurch and walk slowly up to the vehicle. Here is Amadou Tall. We are back to our old vehicle, which has been mended. He shakes our hands with the enthusiasm of long parting.

'I have been waiting,' he says, grinning. 'The Toyota is fixed.' And, indeed, the vehicle fires on first attempt and we are off, following the beams of our headlights across the dark countryside.

In Kaédi we stop briefly at Monsieur Po's, to drop him off and to meet up with Mustapha, our old driver, whom we need to pay. Mustapha is smiling and cheerful and gives me such a very warm and impassioned thank you that I see, contrary to impressions, we have indeed made an impact on him.

The journey back to Keniéba feels long and it is with tremendous relief that I eventually collapse into bed in my hut.

9 Among the Pastoralists

An encounter with the police... The True Peul... In defense of tractors... Why teenage boys must work... Siting future wells... The sacrilege of selling cattle... Artistic herders... Heroic well-diggers... A dispute over donkeys... A lost herd

We are going out to Bokel Djouli today, a pastoralists' encampment a little to the north where we are in the process of digging a well. We will pass the night there. This is a favored spot of mine. I especially like to be amongst the pastoralists on their empty plains, and Bokel Djouli is the home of a particular friend. But we had a long day of it yesterday and will not head out until later on. So, for the larger part of the morning, I lounge about my room, going through a few papers with Salif, dozing and shooing away flies. We eat an early meal at midday and drink a quick succession of teas; then we are off.

It is early afternoon and the hottest time of day. The town is quiet, people sheltering from the fierce sunlight like mariners from a storm. We pass up over the road following a sandy track northwards through a scattering of Moorish encampments. To my surprise, just as we are leaving the last of these behind, we pass a police post and are called to a halt. This is unusual, as there are not normally such posts in this area.

The two police officers at the post look surly and one of them heads over to us. He asks for my passport and takes it over to his companion, who studies it closely. Soon they are back at the vehicle. What am I doing here? Where is my *mission*, my signed document stating my purpose and employment? Whose vehicle are we travelling in? They are aggressive and seem suspicious of me. Salif tells them that the Adjutant is aware of our movements, as he has just called him, but this does not seem to impress the men. They are police, not gendarmes.

I do not have a *mission*, as I always travel to Mauritania on a tourist visa. I have long been aware that, were I to seek official status in the country by registering with the relevant ministry to conduct development activities, this might well undermine the work Salif and I do. We would then most likely find it hard to avoid working in conjunction with some government agency not of our choice, which could then claim ownership of at least a part of the work we do, leaving us prey to exploitation. Only last year, we narrowly avoided something like this happening. A government agency for water and hydraulics got wind of the fact that Salif was involved in well digging at our project in Bokel Djouli, which at that time was still at the planning stage. The director of the agency, a Moor of some influence in the region, got a message through to Salif saying that he could not go ahead with the well digging without his permission and without the involvement of his agency. This, Salif knew well, was shorthand for saying that, if the director did not get a cut of the action, he would prevent the work from going ahead. Salif had no choice but to take the matter to the regional Prefect, hoping he would find in Salif's, rather than the agency director's, favor. To give him his credit, this is what the man duly did, saying the director's permission was not required, and we were able to go ahead with the well without interference. But it was a close-run thing and illustrated clearly the benefits – at least in the current state of affairs in southern

Mauritania – of keeping our heads below the parapet.

Having received my somewhat vague replies to their questions about my lack of *mission*, the two soldiers go off again, still in possession of my passport. A long period ensues. Has my long period of anonymity finally come to an end in southern Mauritania? We sit patiently, stewing in the heat. Then one of the soldiers finally emerges, saunters slowly over to where we are parked, and, with a nod, hands me back my passport. They were probably just bored.

There are three predominant types of terrain in the region of southern Mauritania in which we work. There are the lower-lying flood plains of the Moshe and Senegal rivers, where the majority of the agriculture takes place and where the towns of Keniéba and Kaédi, as well as many villages, are to be found. To the south are sandy, more elevated lands, also containing many villages, some parts of which are still well forested, the tall, thorny trees creating a canopy that in places is almost complete. To the north, meanwhile, is the land of the pastoralists. Here there is the same, more elevated sandy terrain, but the trees are gone and the vast stretches of open country – in some places rising to plateaus of black, gravelly rubble; in others falling to wide expanses of soft sand – run unheeded to a horizon not far beyond which is the true desert.

This is a land of bleached straw-grass, barren plains, mud-hut and thorn-stick villages that are little more than herders' encampments, and a sky that at times is a dome of blue, and at others an unglimpsable sheet of fire. So inhospitable can this country be that those who live in it are either there because over the centuries they have become highly adapted to its conditions, or because they are poor and marginalized and this barren area is all that is left to them. Those from this last group come mostly from the Harratin community: the Black Moors, descended from freed slaves, many of whom occupy the position of the lowest status and privilege in the country. The first group, those who have long been in the region and are highly adapted to living in it, constitute the core of Peul society: the *Vrai Peul*, or True Peul, as Salif calls them. Traditionally, these cattle-breeding livestock herders would have been semi-nomadic: affiliated to 'home' villages where the Qur'anic schools, markets and the larger family were to be found, but for most of the year following the rains and pastures with their herds. When on the move they would have lived in camps in the countryside, some only temporary structures for groups of young men on the move, others more substantial villages where families would remain on a semi-permanent basis.

Today, this pattern has changed, for it was these people who were most affected by the great droughts of the 1970s and early 1980s, with most of their livestock perishing. Many went to the towns, never to return, and those who remain have greatly reduced herds and these days rely more on the seasonal crops they plant and the extra animals they tend for the 'town' families. This has resulted in their lifestyles becoming more settled and their camps more permanent. Young men will still travel far with their livestock, when necessary going south even into Mali to find pastures, but life is harder now. The pools upon which they water their animals – left in riverbeds after the rains – now dry up much quicker, or never form at all; pastures are thinner and are more rapidly exhausted; crops are harder to cultivate; and the cost of living has gone up, meaning the herders get relatively less money now for their animals. But the Vrai Peul are indomitable, proud people, and I have always found their dignity and independence of spirit inspiring. They are tall, fair-skinned and fine-boned, and they step across the wide expanses of their country in the wake of their white, scimitar-horned cattle as though the rest of the world did not exist.

Amadou Tall is in his element as we head north into this

land of sand and scrub: he drives much better off-road than on. We traverse a few deep *oueds* of soft sand despite the fact that we are still in two-wheel drive mode, the engagement of four-wheel drive being reserved, in traditional manner, for only once one has already become stuck. To me, it seems like we drive with randomness, ranging widely across the difficult country, swivelling frequently through 90 or even 180 degrees in order to find a route. But this is highly familiar territory to Amadou Tall and Salif, my companions, who themselves come originally from a Vrai Peul family. Before long we have made our way to an expansive area of arable fields. These are the traditional rain-fed fields of a number of semi-pastoral families who, during the rainy season, set up small camps nearby. People are working the land, breaking it up with hoes in preparation for the rains and the planting of the millet crop. In one area, Salif's development group's tractor is at work, ploughing. This is what we have come to see and we walk over to where the owner of the land is standing.

The farmer is a stocky man in a white tunic, a turban loosely piled on top of his head. In his hands is a hoe, as he has been working at some soil lumps left behind by the tractor. He is sweating profusely and straightens up to greet us. Salif asks him how the work is going.

'It's good,' he says in surprisingly proficient French. 'The tractor is very good.'

'How much does it help you?' I ask him. I still have to answer that vexing question of whether or not we are encouraging an unsustainable form of agriculture by providing access to our tractor for ploughing.

'The tractor,' the man replies, enunciating the words carefully now, as though he knows what is in my mind, 'is six times more economical than working the land by hand.'

'That is a lot,' I say. I ask him to explain how this comes about.

'We get much better yields,' the man says. 'Last year, for

example, I only managed to plough half my land with the tractor, and the half I did by hand produced nothing... nothing, I tell you. The rains were weak last year and so the water did not lie on the ground long enough for it to penetrate the soil. But on the land worked by the tractor,' he continues proudly, 'the ground is so well broken that the water penetrates deeply and we get good crops. Tractors,' he finishes, 'are very good.' I suspect it might not only be because he speaks good French that Salif has brought me to this man.

We walk over to where people are digging the land with hoes: these are the fields for which there is not sufficient money to hire the tractor. It is tough work, as the ground is baked hard. Most of those working are boys and young men, as it is for this category of males, between the ages of about 10 and 18, that the lion's share of the hardest manual labor is reserved. According to Mamadou, Salif's cousin back in the compound, this is because they are 'closer to the ground' and so do not have to bend so far. I have always found it interesting how, in contrast to the developed world, where a man's physical working prime is reckoned to be somewhere in his mid to late twenties, here it is early youth that represents the physical resource of most value. From around the age of 20, a young man might be free to go off 'on adventure', or to seek local employment that will allow him to start raising the money he will need to get married. But before that, his vitality and durability are fully exploited: he is expected to work. And surely it does help that, at the beginning at least, he is 'closer to the ground'.

The speed and efficiency with which the tractor shears through the hard soil, when compared with the laborious, meter-by-meter task of working it by hand, speaks volumes on the subject of modernization versus traditional farming methods. Of course, there are all sorts of issues involved in mechanization, including the problems of soil run-off and nutrient depletion, but, watching the boys break the soil for crops that may well simply wilt or become prey to birds, locusts or the ever-threatening camels – and anyway will at best not produce a yield sufficient to support families – I cannot help sympathizing with the desire to move beyond subsistence farming. As Ibrahim Tandia said: African agriculture must develop.

We range widely over the countryside in search of four villages that have been selected as possible locations for further wells. The digging of wells is a new area for Salif and me, and reflects perhaps our natural liking for these pastoral peoples who, along with their poorer Harratin neighbors, have always seemed to me the most marginalized of communities. They demand little and so get little. They have little or no representation, even at local level. Governments and authorities have long seen pastoralists as little more than a nuisance, as, by the nature of their mobile lifestyles and independence of mind, they are harder to control. But in marginal lands such as these, the ability to move about and mix agriculture with animal husbandry is perhaps the best way forward.

The main problem the people from this region have is

simply a lack of access to clean drinking water. Often, they will have to travel 10 kilometers to their nearest permanent source of water, which is likely to be of poor quality. Periodically, a government agency that has won a grant or been allocated some funds will show up and dig a well or sink half a dozen boreholes. But these projects are generally conducted with such an eye to what monies can be creamed off into the pockets of their managers and directors that the work is done poorly and the wells and boreholes do not function properly. So we decided we would help to dig some wells, starting with the one at Bokel Djouli, which is already under way. Meanwhile, Salif has been busy canvassing other communities and commissioning hydrological surveys, because, at 40 or 50 meters, the water table is deep, and we want to be sure of finding water.

The four villages consist of collections of well-established Peul herder camps, 500-600 people strong, although a couple have adjoining camps of Harratin as well. Peul herder camps are different from other villages. For starters, as opposed to the rectangular, mud-brick style of construction typical across much of Mauritania, they favor the cooler, round, thatched hut, the wooden frame of which is plastered in a smooth render of cow dung and mud: textured and attractive. Here and there they are painted in simple geometric patterns, and, instead of being huddled all together in tight, interlocking networks, as in the other villages, they stand a little apart from each other, giving a sense of space and openness.

We do not stay long in each village: just long enough to locate the village chief, have a brief look about and confirm details such as the number of inhabitants and the distance to current water sources, these being some of the criteria upon which each village was selected. One of the villages has a borehole where a number of women are working at a treadle pump, pumping the foot pedal up and down, two at a time. It is hard work and produces only a thin stream of water.

Perhaps inevitably, there are problems with the pump, which needs a new part, but this is only obtainable in Nouakchott, many hundreds of kilometers away. The women work the pump continuously all day long and well into the night in order to fulfil the village's domestic water needs. I have a go at the pump myself, much to the amusement of the women. It is hard work pushing it down, and I can see why they do it two at a time.

We are seated on a spread of mats in the shade of a hut: Salif, myself, an old village chief and a number of other men. Around us are dotted further round huts, beyond which stretch the golden plains. The men are dressed in *bobos* and turbans, their sandals scattered around the edges of the mats, their roughened hands and feet, idle for the moment, poised and sculptural. There is a question I want to ask, although I am aware it might cause some controversy. Salif translates for me.

'You number here some 500 people, split between four camps,' I say. There is a murmur of agreement. 'You have 150 cows and 280 sheep and goats.' Heads shake in agreement. 'Your nearest source of permanent water is the Mabafe, six kilometers away.'

I pause a moment, then ask: 'What is the current value of a reasonable-quality bullock?'

A discussion ensues, resulting in a figure Salif relates to me that is roughly the equivalent of $400. This is a lot, as I expected.

'You have told me you need veterinary medicines,' I continue, 'and that your borehole needs fixing; you would like to have a well.' I pause. 'Why don't you sell some of your cattle to pay for some of these things? Only one or two head would do. Over time, you could even probably pay for the construction of a well.'

Salif is smiling. The men look at each other, unsure how to

take this; some also smiling.

'It is a good question,' one of them says in French.

There is a well-known Peul saying to the effect that 'the Peul never sell their cattle'. I quote this to them now, asking if this is the reason, and they laugh, as they can see now that I am not a complete idiot; that I am not making a 'serious' proposition: how could I be? Should a man be expected to sell his inheritance; dispose of his heirlooms? For this, more than anything else, is what the cattle herds represent to the Peul.

But of course it *was* a serious question. They will not go against this deeply embedded instinct to preserve their herds, an instinct that will prohibit them from parting with any significant part of them to alleviate even life-or-death situations. But perhaps, if Ibrahim Tandia's plan comes to fruition, we can sow the tiniest seed of such an idea. Because, if they want to survive, they, like everyone else, are going to have to adapt the way they think and operate. That is the new reality.

We pass a number of Harratin villages and I ask Amadou Tall to pull up at one of them. Ever since my earliest days in Mauritania, wandering in the desert amongst the Moors, I have had a soft spot for the Harratin, the Black Moors. Being descended from slaves captured by the White Moors centuries ago – and also freed long ago – they are a community with the lowest 'caste' status in Mauritania. Not all are poor or powerless, and they constitute the majority of the country's urban population. Even one or two government ministers come of Harratin stock. But of all the marginalized, dispossessed peoples in the country, it is the rural-dwelling, small-scale animal-herding, Harratin families who stand out the most.

These people have long ago been abandoned by White Moorish society with its strong families, clans and regional affiliations. They have long lost any connection to the original

Bantu Black peoples from which they came, with their all-encompassing cultural traditions and wide networks of connections and loyalties. They wander the barren fringes of the desert with only the weakest ties to the land, with little history or tradition, and with only a handful of livestock. They have no *patron* families or 'home' villages or tribal support networks.

Those I came across in my wanderings lived under scraps of tents, tending threadbare patches of crops when the rains allowed, only surviving with the greatest difficulty. When I came to them, they would invite me to stay the night. I would be given hospitality and companionship, despite their great shyness of me. Their children – weak, naked and begrimed – would cry at the sight of me. Their exhausted wives, worn down by toil by the age of 20, went trancelike through the motions of accommodating me. And the menfolk were monosyllabic. But always I felt behind this their great desire to give to me, to share with me, as this – to give and share – was about all they had left.

We pull up beside the scrappy collection of mud buildings. The place looks windblown and deeply impoverished. A few numb-looking children stare at us. Then, an old man in the rags of a *bobo* appears. His face is a ravage of pockmarks and destroyed teeth. Soon other men appear. They look a desperate sight: ragged, disfigured, coughing deep chesty coughs. I am a little shocked at the pitiful state of the place, especially when compared with the neighboring Peul villages that always maintain, despite their poverty, a neat, cared-for aspect.

Salif greets the men in Hassaniya, the Moorish language. He asks them a few friendly questions, but then reverts to ritualistic greetings, as I have not mentioned any particular reason as to why I wanted to stop here. I am not quite sure myself. The old man with the pockmarked face offers me a greeting. I reply rather weakly with the query: '*Ça va? Ça*

va?'– Okay?

'*Ça va pas,*' the old man immediately retorts back in French. '*Je n'ai pas du manger, ni d'argent, ni de vêtements. Bien sûr, ça va pas*' – I do not have any food, nor any money, nor any clothes. Of course I am not okay.

I do not know how to respond to this, but the old man is speaking to Salif now. 'He says can we dig them a well,' Salif says. The old man speaks some more. 'He says that if we do this, Allah will smile on us always.' The old man speaks again. 'With a well, he says, they will live like princes.'

'Has this village been considered as one of the possible sites for a well?' I ask.

'Yes, it was considered,' Salif replies, 'but it was not chosen.'

'Why not?'

'Because the people are too disorganized,' he says. 'They would not be able to form a committee and they could not decide what contribution they would give the well-digging team.' These are two of the further criteria a village needs to fulfil in order to be chosen: that they show the ability to participate in the well digging and that they form a group to manage the hygienic use of the well afterwards. Apparently, this community is not up to this. The old man grins at me toothlessly. The others stare implacably.

We do not remain in the village long after this. There is little we can do here. I feel impotent as we drive away; frustrated that, for the moment at least, there is nothing we can offer these people.

A dry riverbed: men drawing water from temporary wells dug into its surface. These are the inhabitants of Bokel Djouli, which is nearby, and, at this time of the year when the countryside is at its driest, this is where they get their water. The wells, perhaps a dozen in all, consist of pits three to five meters deep. Men stripped to the waist stand at the top of a number of them with long poles over their shoulders. At the end of each pole hangs a water container made from a car tire's inner tube. A man will let the inner tube drop into a pit where another submerges it in the small pool of water that has accumulated there. Using the weight of the other end of the pole as a counter lever, the first man then swings the inner tube up and, with a series of practiced movements, pours its contents into a number of plastic water containers waiting to be loaded onto donkeys for the journey home.

The first person to greet us is my friend Moussa, a tall man with an afro and eyes of the deepest black. His naked torso is streaming with sweat from his exertions at the wells and he greets us with the warm, wry smile and glint of humor in his eye by which I always remember him. His French is excellent.

'You are to spend the night. That is good,' he says. 'We have already selected a goat for you' – this, in reference to the animal that will be slaughtered in my honor despite my annual insistence that this is not necessary. 'We have chosen a good fat one,' he smiles.

Every day at this time of year, Moussa and his companions come here, digging the wells ever deeper and drawing off the water that has accumulated in them since their last visit. It is backbreaking work but Moussa seems always to go at it with relish. I have never heard him complain, even though each year when the rains come, the wells collapse and need to be dug all over again. The water that comes from them is also of poor quality, as livestock pollute it, and dirt and scraps continually fall into them. Indeed, Moussa himself only last year was the victim of such a bad waterborne infection that, had it not been for his quick thinking and Salif's prompt actions, he would have certainly died. Severe vomiting at night was the first indication that something was wrong. By morning, he was delirious, with extreme stomach cramps. Knowing that this was not one of the ordinary stomach complaints with which he and his family were only too familiar, he managed to call Salif on his mobile phone. Salif immediately sent the Toyota to fetch him and, when he arrived in Keniéba, decided to send him straight on to Nouakchott, as it was well known that the hospital in Kaédi was badly understaffed and people sometimes had to wait days there before being seen. It must have been a desperate journey to Nouakchott, Moussa deteriorating in the back seat through all those long hours. But eventually they arrived and found a doctor, who said that Moussa's infection and its resulting complications were so bad that he would certainly have died had he not received such prompt attention.

Moussa is to remain at the wells and meet us at Bokel Djouli later on. We drive on and arrive at the village, which consists of four Peul herder camps. Each camp is separated from its neighbor by several hundred meters, and each is encircled by a wide band of dried cattle dung, for it is around each collection of huts that the livestock gather at night: close and intimate. The camps themselves are surrounded by simple stick fences inside which the earth is scraped clean and in places plastered in the same smooth render as the huts. These last, and especially those of Salim's camp, are the most comfortable and pretty constructions I have ever seen in Mauritania where, on the whole, styles of accommodation rarely aspire beyond the utilitarian.

Here, the render of the huts is worked in such a fashion as to give them a beautifully finished, 'earthenware' look, with rounded doorways, tiny, triangular windows and 'hems' as seamlessly attached to the smoothed earth upon which they stand as anthills. It is the insides of the huts which most impress, though. Here, again, the neatness and attention to detail goes well beyond the purely utilitarian. Geometric patterns are painted on the walls, and possessions – some packed in trunks, some hanging from pegs, some displayed on long shelves – are arranged with the care of a shrine. The center of each hut is taken up by a large wooden dais covered in mats and cushions and on the walls are pinned photographs of friends and relations, poignant reminders of people from far away and long ago: smart young men, full of hope in some distant city; highly dressed women with the fear of the camera in their eyes; almost completely faded ancients. It is the sense of pride and care inherent in these huts and camps that strikes one. The people may have little, but they still believe in themselves; they are unbroken.

Moussa has two wives, both friendly, pretty and hard working; each with a hut of her own. He has five daughters and, to his relief I imagine, an infant son. The relief would not be because Moussa in any way regrets his many daughters – he patently adores them – but simply because women do not tend livestock and, if he does not want the entire burden of this falling on his shoulders as he gets older, he must have some sons.

We are greeted at the camp and mats are spread for us in the shade of one of the huts. Before we settle down, however, we make our way towards one of the neighboring camps, near to which is the well we are digging.

The digging of this well has been long and painful. This is partly because it is the first one we have dug and so there has been a steep learning curve. It is also to do with the fact that we have encountered a band of hard rock, reducing the rate of progress at times to a meter a fortnight. For five months already, from the end of the last rainy season, all through the dry season and now into the beginning of the hot season, the well-digger and his team have been hard at it. Another reason why the work has been so problematic, however, is because we decided to follow the route of an old, defunct well, reasoning that at least then we would be sure of striking water. As this well, though, had originally been poorly constructed, failing even to be sunk at a true perpendicular and having large cavities in its sidewalls, this has proved difficult, in essence requiring the meter-by-meter deconstruction of the existing well, all concrete and steel reinforcing rods included. And all this has been accomplished without the use of power tools; all has been done with hammer and chisel. This is not how it should be and lessons have been learned.

In my opinion, the well-digger – who is a local professional – and his team are nothing short of heroic. Salif tells me that few people would stick it out with the conditions they have had to put up with: over-long exposure to extreme heat and isolation; an inadequacy of tools; and a vastly overrun schedule. It is Salif's gift that he is able to pick out such people.

Ahmedou Soro, the well-digger, is a softly spoken, middle-aged man with the demeanor of a hermit or monk. Back and forth from the well he leads the donkey, which draws the bucket of rubble up 40 meters on the end of a long piece of rope. The well is beautifully constructed, a meter and a half wide, straight as a die and smoothly lined with steel-reinforced concrete. There is a call from the bottom, and with the next run of the donkey a young man, half-naked and grey with dust, appears swinging from the rope, one foot

in the bucket. His shift in the confined patch at the bottom of the well is over, and he switches with the young man who has been ferrying the rubble away in a wheelbarrow. Under a lean-to nearby, the third member of Ahmedou Soro's team is occupied bending steel-reinforcing rods on a vice. It is physical work, all of it: gruelling and relentless.

Ahmedou Soro cannot leave his donkey, so the next time he comes to a stop at the top of the well I go over to greet him. He is cheerful and polite and I peer into the black depths of the well.

'It's a long way down,' I say. 'How deep do you think you will you have to go?'

'Forty-five meters, possibly more,' he says.

'How long will that take you?'

He thinks a moment. 'It depends on the rock,' he says. 'It could take a further month.' This is a long time and I am just thinking how clearly we cannot continue in this fashion when Ahmedou Soro prompts: 'What we need is a pneumatic drill. With a pneumatic drill the job will go much faster.' I assure him that we will look into it and that if we dig any further wells, we will certainly not do so in the manner we have done this one.

There is another issue I want to ask Ahmedou Soro about, the one concerning the supply of donkeys by the local community. Donkeys are used not only for pulling the rubble out of the well, but also each morning for emptying the water that collects in it overnight. The Bokel Djouli community were supposed to supply these but, amazingly, as comparatively small as this contribution towards the digging of their well is, they have failed to do this consistently and Salif has even had to bring in donkeys from Keniéba. This is doubly incomprehensible considering that herder villages such as these are always well endowed with donkeys, and in fact generally have far more of them than they need. I find this whole issue highly dispiriting. Can these people really be so cavalier about their future that they will not even contribute the small amount that has been asked of them in order to secure something as important to their survival as a permanent supply of water? Am I missing something here? Are Salif and I being taken for a ride? I ask Ahmedou Soro for his view on the matter.

'They are poor people,' he says. 'Perhaps they do not have the donkeys to spare.' This is not good enough for me, I think angrily. They should make sure they have the donkeys to spare. We agreed on this before we started.

We go back to Moussa's camp, where there is now a gathering of people, as Salif has called a meeting of the well committee to see if we can get to the bottom of the matter. Deep down, I suspect there will be a logical answer, as indeed there usually is. But for the moment I am filled with chagrin.

It is evening by now; the light is soft and the shadows long. Moussa has turned up with a couple of other men, and we all settle down on a large spread of mats. Salif does the talking. Yes, it is confirmed that there have indeed been problems supplying donkeys to the well-diggers. Yes, it is understood that the supply of such donkeys was a requirement of the community. A prolonged discussion ensues. The committee consists of six men and two women: a friendly and jolly bunch who I can see are making an effort to lend the issue the importance I am obviously attaching to it. The problem, it emerges at the end of the discussion, is to do with the fact that there was not sufficient pasture near to the village this year as a result of the poor rains, meaning the donkeys had to be sent off and so were not available to the well-diggers. This is still not good enough for me.

'But that is their concern,' I say to Salif. 'They agreed that they would provide the donkeys and so they should have found a way to do this. They could have brought fodder to them here, for example.' Salif translates this and the committee members again plunge into voluble discussion.

'It is true,' one of them eventually says, 'we failed to provide the donkeys. We would have brought fodder to them here, but by then we had no fodder left.' Perhaps, I think to myself, this is it: these people simply do not have the resources to contribute even the small amount of help we have asked for. Perhaps we should not have even asked for it in the first place, even though it is important that communities show commitment to their well by contributing to its construction, as it is through such a commitment that they demonstrate their ability to run and maintain a well for the benefit of the larger community. I am just starting to think that this must be the explanation, or one that is going to have to be good enough anyway, when Moussa, who all along has been sitting a little apart petting a young daughter curled, feline-like, in his lap, interjects: 'If I may say something?'

'Of course,' Salif replies.

'I think the main problem here is one of misunderstanding,'

he says, speaking to me in French, which most present do not understand.

'The people here do not understand about charities and aid agencies,' he goes on. 'They think anyone involved in aid or development is part of the government and will therefore naturally be defrauding any project they are involved with. Many of them,' he says with a smile, 'even think Salif here is making money out of this well. Why should they contribute towards the well, then, they think to themselves, if it is only helping to enrich others?'

'And what about those who do not think this?' I ask.

'It is difficult,' he says. 'It is difficult to get people to provide donkeys when some refuse.'

'Hmm,' I reply, not entirely satisfied with this answer either.

'Do not think that there have not been any donkeys supplied,' Salif chips in now. 'It is just that there were not enough and the ones we had got tired. The committee assures me this will not happen again.'

And so we leave it at that. Somewhere in the gulf between the expectations and requirements of the Western funder and the on-the-ground reality for the African receiver – an inherently undesirable and, in fact, I believe, quite misunderstood relationship – lies the truth. It is a meeting point that will never satisfy either but, for the moment, in such situations, is better than nothing.

A sun flattening on the horizon: in a moment it is gone and soon fingers of dusk are creeping over the land. The livestock arrive home shortly before dark – great herds of sheep and goats rustling softly over the ground like a thousand leaves. Kids and lambs are released and for a while their and their mothers' cries drown out all else as they hunt for each other amongst the milling herds. The cattle arrive last, like long-range explorers, plodding their slow, inexorable pace along paths worn onto the

dry earth. They make their way to the camp where in a mass they stand chewing the cud or settle their large carcasses down like boulders. Moussa, now finished with the meeting, which has broken up, wanders amongst them with a small stool under his arm and a bowl in his hand. The cattle shake their wide, scimitar horns, flick a tail; scratch a white flank with a hoof. They are peaceful, unhurried; majestic. Moussa steps amongst them like a heron amongst the rocks on the seashore. He finds the ones he is looking for, quickly hobbles them and squats down on his stool for a brief milking.

Watching darkness come over this pastoral land, and watching the herds of livestock settle down for the night, is deeply soothing. It is as if the world were sighing, letting out a deep breath: the sound and smell of animals all around; the greying distances; the pretty mud huts perched on their scraped patches of earth, here and there the glint of a cooking fire now visible; the naked children still playing in the last of the light; the women clanking pots as they prepare the evening meal. There is something about the pastoral life, linked as it is to the rhythms and pace of its livestock, enacted under the great arch of the heavens, that draws me in. If there were one place on the globe I would call the home and hearth of humanity, it would be here: somewhere where life is closest to being uncluttered and elemental.

We are to eat a goat but the preparation of it, I notice, has not yet even started. Indeed, it has not yet even been killed but is bleating pathetically at a peg nearby, awaiting its fate. This Moussa seals once he has finished with the livestock. To the light of torches, the beast is held down, its head facing east to Mecca, while its throat is swiftly cut and its blood and life drained away. Now it is hung from a post for Moussa expertly to strip down and butcher. The women receive the cuts into pots already boiling. Choice bits will be roasted. We are to have a feast, and I am glad to see there are quite a number present, as my stomach, which is always troublesome, will not put up with much. The evening is long and dark. Those around me are in cheerful moods, and the conversation is lively. I lie back listening to the babble of conversation, watching the stars. Dish after dish of the goat comes: roasted, boiled, on a bed of couscous, with some salad even.

Later, in the darkness that falls like a cloak all around us, Moussa tells a story. It is for my benefit, clearly, as he speaks in French.

'We used to have great herds here,' he says. 'So vast we could not count them. But when the big droughts came our lives changed forever.'

'I was a boy at that time,' he goes on. 'The droughts lasted many years and it was hard for us. We sent animals east and west in search of pastures. My father even knew of places to the north where grasses could be found in the driest years, and at that time there were also many more trees whose seeds we could feed to the animals. But it was hard.'

We are silent as we sit under the stars listening, even those – the majority – who cannot understand French.

'For a long time, though, we lost only the weakest of our beasts. This was because my father was a good herder and understood about livestock health. Then, one year towards the end, the drought gripped even tighter and it was at this moment that my father decided to send the cattle south into Mali. We had not yet sent the cattle south, as that was where everyone was heading and there was much competition over the few pastures there were there. But by now we were losing beasts at a fast rate, and to have any hope of saving those that remained my father saw that he had no choice. There was nothing left in Mauritania.'

'My brother at that time,' Moussa continues, 'was a young man of 17 or 18 and my father decided that it would be he who would take the cattle south. He himself did not want to leave the family, as we were all suffering at that time, and he knew we needed his support. So my brother, Mohamed, took the beasts south with the aid of two young cousins. They went into Mali, where we heard from someone that they had found some grazing. Then all went silent. Six months passed, and we heard nothing. Eight months passed, and my father set out with his brother to see if he could find them. They too were gone a long time.

'I was about 12 then, and it was up to me to look after the family while my father was away, as my brother and I were his only sons. We were living in Keniéba at that time, as there was nothing for us in the countryside. All our livestock were dead except one bull and a handful of sheep and goats, which we had somehow managed to keep alive. It was at this time I started going to school.

'My father came home after two months and told us that Mohamed and our two cousins who had gone with him were dead. We could not believe it and we were deeply grieved.

They had been killed, my father said, in a skirmish with some villagers.

'My father had not gone to the village where they had been killed,' Moussa continues, his voice low now but still clear in the darkness of the night, 'as he was warned that, if he did so, the villagers might grow angry with him and do him some harm. Their bodies, he was told, had been burned.

'Apparently, the villagers claimed that it was they who had first been attacked. The villagers, my father was told, had gone to complain to my brother and some other herders who were with him at that time that they had not paid the price they had agreed upon for some fields of millet stalks the villagers were allowing their cattle to graze. My brother and the other herders, it was said, had refused to give up the goats that had been agreed as the price and had attacked them with knives. The deaths occurred when the villagers retaliated and a battle ensued.

'But later on my father heard a different version of this story from one of the herders who had been with my brother but had escaped. According to this boy, although a price of some goats had indeed been agreed upon for the grazing, the villagers increased this price every day, eventually refusing my brother and the herders access to the village wells unless they gave over half their cattle in payment. When my brother and the other herders refused this, the villagers came to them in the fields in numbers, armed with machetes and even some old guns, and it was then that the battle ensued which resulted in the deaths. The cattle, the boy said, were stolen and sold.

'The matter was looked into by the authorities, but at that time there was such turmoil and destitution in the Sahel, with people dying of hunger every day, that the case was never cleared up. Mohamed was my elder brother and so from that time on, with the exception of my father, I was the eldest male in the family. And that,' Moussa says, that glint of humor I know him by so well now again visible in his eye, 'as everyone knows, means lots of responsibility.'

I sleep that night on a mat under the stars. Salif and Amadou Tall opt for the inside of a hut and so, once everyone else has gone to bed, I am alone. I wrap a sheet about myself and for a long time I just lie, listening to the silence. Somewhere far off on the plain a pack of dogs is howling. Later, a donkey brays, loud and painful. I wake many times that night, and at each waking wonder for a moment where I am; then, as I see the stars overhead, remembrance washes over me like a cool breeze.

10 A Day of Wind

The redundancy of dogs... The value of a fence... Culture and money... Donkey ploughs and microcredit... The selflessness of Salif and Mariam... An audience with the Mayor... Classroom floors and blackboards... The ancient hunter

First thing in the morning, Moussa is out amongst his herds. He wanders through the sheep and goats, slowly circling after the kids and lambs, for whose hind legs he makes sudden lunges. Soon he has a handful of each dangling from his hands like fruits. Meanwhile, a rampant donkey is attempting to mount its not-very-willing mate. Hooves flash like gunshots and long, yellow teeth are bared. A billy goat is pursuing one of its vast harem, groaning in the throes of pheromonal ecstasy. The cattle, earliest of risers, are long gone.

I am always pleased to see the dogs, which slink about the edges of the camp. They are always of the same sleek, long-legged, hunting-dog model, as though this is the final mongrel conclusion. Their heads are small and their white, shorthaired coats are splattered with brown, and, it seems to me, there is always a smile on their faces. This is surprising, as they do not have very good lives. In fact, I have never quite understood why they exist at all. Their role as protectors is more or less redundant, as livestock raiders here are pretty much a thing of the past, and all wild animals of any size have long been wiped out in Mauritania. And yet every herder camp has any number of dogs dashing territorially about, and they can also be found in villages and towns throughout the country. No-one, as far as I can see, feeds them, except perhaps periodically throwing them a bone or some leftovers. They are emaciated, flea-ridden and frequently disabled from fights. Never have I seen a human touch one or in fact pay the slightest attention to them beyond hurling the odd stone. And yet still they smile, confident deep down, one feels, that they remain 'man's best friend'.

Today will be a day of wind. By early morning, gusts of stinging dust are swirling around and the sky is grey, as though overcast. We take our leave of Moussa and his family promptly. We leave them standing in a family group inside the little fence that surrounds their camp: tall Moussa with a child in his arms; two or three young, pretty girls smiling confidently; his two wives, waving.

Salif and Amadou Tall are in a cheerful mood as we head out, inspired perhaps by the the plains of the Vrai Peul calling to their pastoralist heritage.

'It is a good day,' Amadou Tall shouts over the noise of the wind, despite evidence to the contrary.

'We will go to the south,' Salif replies. 'It will not take us long. We will finish by midday.' His face is lit and happy and unusually carefree.

Today is my last day before we return to Nouakchott and we still have a number of tasks to accomplish with some farmers with whom we are working in the south.

In a couple of hours we are in different country. Here we are amongst trees; tall thorny trees that in places almost meet overhead. In the old days a lot of the region was like this, and it's said you could travel to Kaédi from many parts of it without once having to leave the shade of the trees. What it is that has protected these trees where elsewhere they have disappeared, I am not sure. Perhaps the communities here are more organized and have been able to prevent the villagers and commercial charcoal burners from cutting them down. Perhaps the authorities have been more resolute in applying the anti-deforestation laws. Or perhaps the lie of the land is such that the trees were more able to tap a water table that had not fallen too deep. Whichever is the case, it is a pleasure to be amongst trees again.

I ask Amadou Tall whether there are any wild animals left here.

'Many,' he replies with a confidence of which I am doubtful. 'There are baboons, which eat the villagers' maize. And hyena. Many others.'

'Have you seen them?' I ask.

'No, no, I haven't seen them, but it is said a hyena took some lambs near Djente village this year.'

'When we were children we saw baboons often,' Salif says diplomatically, 'and there were antelope everywhere. Now, though...' He does not go on and I can understand why. There are no large animals left now. Those not killed by the droughts have either been hunted out or simply shot by communities for whom the bigger species of wildlife represent only a threat. Indeed, the only time I did see a sizable animal anywhere near here, a baboon crossing a road in northern Senegal, the driver of the vehicle in which I was travelling instantly screeched to a halt, grabbed a pistol from under his seat and wildly let fire at it through the window, deafening us both in the process.

Of the smaller examples of wildlife, there is still a certain amount remaining. Now and again on our long drives across even the driest country, I have seen desert hares, with their large, veined ears that act as cooling systems. I have seen pale desert foxes, squirrels and rodents of many types. There are partridge and quail and other small birds whose names I do not know. And often, circling on the thermals far above, are harriers. But the larger animals, I suspect, are the stuff now only of story and rumor.

It is in this forested area that, some years ago, the marginality of the whole region was brought home to me. It was December, the cool, dry season, and, almost without precedent for that time of year, it rained. It was not a large amount of rain, but neither was it a shower: perhaps 300 millimeters over a couple of days. What was remarkable about this was how it affected both people and livestock. Already the cool season, the rain made it even cooler, temperatures dropping to five degrees, which, along with the dampness, caused widespread deaths among herds of sheep unable to cope with exposure to even such mildly adverse conditions. I came across them in the woods: groups of otherwise quite healthy-looking beasts lying dead on the sand. Even some people died from exposure, their bodies unable to cope with the unfamiliar cold. Truly, I realized, this was a region where the line between survival and death is very thin.

The villages in the area we have come to are more substantial than elsewhere. They have proper mosques painted in bright colors, marketplaces, even the odd shop. Now and again a vehicle passes through. They are like smaller versions of Keniéba: networks of sandy passageways and compounds. Fields of millet lie about them, and herds of sheep and goats drift over the surrounding countryside like cloud shadows. To the north is a long depression where, for 15 kilometers, millet is planted as the rainy season floodwaters recede. This is the primary agricultural land for the region and we have been involved in helping to put up a fence to protect some of it from livestock. We drive now to this fence, which does not look particularly remarkable but, Salif assures me, makes a huge difference to the villagers' lives, concentrations of livestock in the south, which is comparatively humid, having increased so much. Salif tells me that last year, before the fence was started, only 2,000 of the 10,000 hectares it will eventually enclose were planted. This year, even though the fence is not yet completed, 4,000 hectares have been sown. This, I think to myself, must be one of the most painless and cost-effective forms of assistance we have given to date. I am even assured by Salif, who has conducted a consultation with the communities involved, that the pastoralists will also benefit from it, as large areas of pasture within the fencing will be protected from over-grazing.

'But what of the Harratin and White Moor animal herders?' I ask, for they too both bring livestock into the area and will probably be less welcome within the fenced area. Salif gives me a weary look.

'It is not a problem,' he says. 'There are ways for them to get through. It is their camels that cause much of the problem.'

I am straying into difficult territory here, I know, as it is this issue – the conflict of interests between the Black African farmers and semi-nomadic Moorish livestock herders – that is and always has been one of the main points of contention between the two communities. The Moors, a confident, bright, opportunistic desert people, descend south as the

pastures wither further north and graze their animals on the high-ground pastures where grazing rights are free to all. They also negotiate with the villagers for access to fields of crop residues where the dung of their animals adds to the soil fertility. But of course it does not always work as smoothly as this and progressively, as the Moors descend south in larger numbers, often settling there for good, the grounds for contention between the two communities grow, with crops being damaged by badly supervised livestock, communal pastures being stripped too early on in the season and land-tenure issues arising.

We proceed to a village where we are proposing to work with a women's co-operative on a small vegetable-growing scheme. Although similar in some ways to the Dohley Women's Market Garden Project in that organic farming methods will be employed, this is on a different scale, with water being drawn by hand from a well as opposed to the mechanized irrigation system of Dohley. The co-operative land is a little outside the village in a clearing in the woods: one hectare of vegetable plots surrounded by a fence. There are only a few women about, as it is the end of the main vegetable-growing season and most of the plots have been harvested. I am told that the co-operative consists of 200 women and that they want to increase their land to two hectares. They also need to re-dig their well, for which they are asking us for funding, as in the cool season it runs dry. We wander about looking at a few compost heaps the women have already made under Salif's instructions, and I ask Salif what the costs of the project will be.

'Re-digging the well and extending the fence are the main costs,' he says; then, after making a calculation on his mobile phone, comes up with a figure that is the equivalent of around $1,500. It is my turn to make a calculation. The 200 women of the co-operative come from probably about a hundred different families. This works out at about $15 a

family – say \$20 if one includes various other costs such as seeds and implements. This is hardly a large amount, and again I am confronted by that same question: why is finance being sought from us when it appears quite within the ability of the villagers to pay for the changes themselves?

'If they organized themselves, these women could quite easily pay for this,' I say to Salif, quoting him my figures. The president of the women's co-operative is with us: a tall, tough-looking woman. Salif puts the question to her.

'It could not be done,' she says simply, Salif translating.

'Why not?' I ask.

'They would not pay,' she says.

I look at Salif. 'Why would they not pay? It is not a large amount.'

'They don't have the money,' he says. 'They do not have the cash available. And even if some families did, they would not all, and certainly not all at the same time. Some would pay and some would not, and then there would be problems.'

I understand. It is the same issue as always, one that I seem to be having the greatest difficulty in getting into my head. The problem is not financial but organizational, even hierarchical, or perhaps even more to the point, it is cultural.

There simply is not the hierarchical structure or precedent for the gathering of a communal fund for agricultural use. Certainly, communal funds do exist, for example for the construction and upkeep of mosques. But this is a time-honored practice for a non-profit-making activity. To gather money for what would be a profit-making activity across all the many different families of an entire community has never been done before and would, as everyone knew, be highly problematic. How to co-ordinate the fundraising? Under what or whose authority? What penalties would there be for non-payment? How would profits be split? And the fact is, in the context of the financial pressures all families constantly live under, the money required from each of them is indeed significant. A women's co-operative would never be prioritized to receive such surplus cash – at least not until such schemes could be shown to be worthwhile financially.

In another village, we inspect a donkey plough. Animal traction for working the land is unused here and it was Monsieur Po whose idea it was to produce this plough for farmers to experiment with. The results, I am told, are spectacular. The farmers have found it to be far more economical than working the land in either the traditional manner, by hand, or by tractor, and there is now a great demand for it. Our hope is that farming in this manner might catch on.

We stop at some fields where we are working with farmers on rainwater harvesting, helping them dig small, foot-high barriers across the contours in their fields. A gnarled old farmer points to one side of one of these simple barriers, where the stalks of an already harvested millet crop are small and threadbare, and compares it to the other side of the barrier, where the water was prevented from running away and the stalk density is at least double.

And we go to a village where we have started a small

microcredit program. Microcredit is a proven development tool. Small pots of money are lent to groups of women who then set up and run their own loan schemes, lending small sums to their members for income-generating activities such as vegetable growing, material dyeing or even simply a bit of commerce. The repayment rates are generally exceptionally high and the schemes are seen as a way of stimulating economic activity and helping women who traditionally have poor access to income-generating opportunities. Our scheme has only just got under way, with $3,000 being lent so far to 10 different groups. The main challenge, Salif tells me, is to get the women to engage with the idea: doing business, even at this level, requires a degree of ambition that many of them simply do not have.

The wind is coming and going; hot on the hand like a blow heater and laden with throat-tickling dust. It gusts violently across the landscape, twirling dust devils to life. Next moment there is a lull and all seems calm.

We head back to Keniéba and arrive around midday. I

am feeling exhausted. We install ourselves in Salif's lounge, as outside all is dust and wind. I do not feel well and doze. Later, a platter of food is produced. It is *mafé*, the Senegalese peanut-stew speciality, although when I mention the dish's provenance, Mariam will have none of it.

'Those Wolof know nothing of cuisine,' she says, referring to the predominant Senegalese ethnic group. 'This is a Peul dish.'

'Certainly the Peul make it very well, and differently,' I hastily backtrack. Mamadou is with us.

'This is what we eat during Ramadan,' he says. 'After we have fasted all day, it is nourishing, as it is full of vitamins.'

The food is helping me feel recovered already. I ask Mamadou whether he also gives up drinking water during Ramadan, as is the requirement between sunrise and sunset.

'Mamadou does not even give up food,' Mariam interrupts.

'Ha!' Mamadou exclaims indignantly. 'What are you talking about? I give up food, except when I am working in the fields. A man cannot work physically without sustenance.'

Mariam laughs. 'Salif drinks nothing in Ramadan,' she says to me.

'That must be hard,' I say.

Salif shakes his head. 'It is hard,' he says, 'especially when Ramadan falls in the hot season.'

'But still you do it,' I say.

'Mostly,' he replies.

'And is ill by the end,' Mariam adds indignantly.

Salif looks tired. He is under almost continuous siege from his mobile phone, his family, villagers, farmers and, for the moment of course, me. At times I see the deep weariness on his face, as he is not a natural leader. He is a quiet man, who one feels would prefer a quiet life.

I am wondering about Salif and Mariam. For the last couple of years, on my departure from Mauritania, I have given Salif some money to pay for the making of bricks for the new house I know he wants to build, the first step towards which is to accumulate sufficient of the concrete blocks modern houses are constructed from to make a start. I know for a fact that he has not used this money for bricks, allowing it instead to be absorbed into the ever-pressing financial needs of the larger family. How can you make bricks when someone needs an eye operation? Or when another's roof has caved in? Others manage, but not Salif. Mariam is still waiting for the fridge she has been talking about for a decade, the one I know she so badly wants, as she finds the hot season unbearable and craves the ability to have a cool drink. But Salif and Mariam, I know, are people who do not expect more than that which comes to them. Never have I heard them voice discontent.

Late afternoon: we have a few last tasks to accomplish. We must go to see the town mayor and pay a visit to a primary school that we have been helping. The wind seems to have settled, although the air is still dusty.

We find Demba Mody, the Mayor, in the *Mairie*, in the new part of town. Demba Mody has a difficult job. His responsibilities are heavy and broad, ranging from all matters municipal, to agricultural issues, issues of a traditional nature, all social and inter-community problems and, most importantly, to acting as the link between the lay town community and the military authorities, represented here by the Adjutant. And all this has to be done without the clout of any real power or any of the significant finances that go with it, since both these, as everyone knows, reside firmly in the hands of the military.

Demba Mody is a tall, gruff man with a shaggy head and bloodshot eyes, and he is unashamedly autocratic in wielding what authority he has. This is an effective approach, considering the many conflicting demands of his role, and the fact that he has been repeatedly re-elected as Mayor for more years than I can remember reflects this. I always make a point of paying him a visit when I am in town. This is both because I sympathize with the difficulties he has to face and because, as weak as his real authority is, it would not be wise to ignore him. He is still a man of some personality.

Any number of people can always be found lurking about the dilapidated building that acts as the *Mairie*. Mostly they are petitioners: farmers with complaints about neighbors or seed suppliers; townspeople whose local well has been fouled; householders who need help on any number of issues. A Moorish merchant might be there seeking a signature allowing him to build a whole new row of merchandise stores that the Mayor knows would be illegal due to their obstruction of a thoroughfare but is powerless to stop because the Adjutant has given the enterprise the nod. A group of landowners might be trying to negotiate with the Prefecture a land title but need an affidavit from the Mayor affirming the land in question has been in constant use by them for more than 10 years. Demba Mody is a realist and deals with everything with little preamble. He will listen to the petitions, then make his decisions and move on to the next.

We are greeted at the door to the *Mairie* by Drémis, Salif's cousin from the compound who does a small amount of clerical work for the Mayor, he with the heart condition and complicated love life.

'Ah, Peter, Salif, you are here. The Mayor will be delighted to see you,' he greets us in his trademark booming voice. 'We are very busy with this election, but the Mayor will see you in a moment. Please, sit down. You will only have to wait a few minutes.'

He smiles, his thin, once-round face strained with the effort of remaining the jolly person he is despite the collapse of his body. There are only two chairs in the porch area that acts as foyer to the Mayor's office, and both are taken. Noticing this, Drémis glares at the two farmer-types occupying them and they both graciously get up, offering their places. I at first decline, but Drémis, who insists, is not one to be defeated, so I sit myself down.

'There is a French mission in town,' Drémis says by way of making conversation. 'Have you seen them? French youths... delinquents... fools.'

'What French people?' Salif asks. Neither of us has any idea what he is talking about.

'Ah... the French,' Drémis replies, as though this were enough explanation, but then adds: 'they have come to build a youth center for our young people. It will be very good and have solar panels to run a DVD player or some music. They are young criminals, mad.'

'What do you mean?' Salif says.

'You know,' Drémis replies. 'They are simple.' He taps his head. 'There are others to look after them, and they have come to build the youth center.' No doubt this is some French social rehabilitation scheme.

'What have you been doing today?' I ask Drémis, to change the subject.

'Pah, pah, pah,' he exclaims, 'there is too much to do. The Mayor is standing for re-election. There is much to organize.' At this moment the door to the Mayor's office opens and the Mayor appears, leading a large Moor by the hand. They are finishing their conversation, and take leave of each other with overly loud bonhomie, business completed. Demba Mody sees us.

'Monsieur Peter, Salif – greetings. Come into my office,' he says with little formality. We are jumping the queue, I know, but I do not feel mentioning this will strike a chord. Demba Mody throws himself behind his large metal desk, and we take a seat on the two chairs across from it that are about the only other things in the room. He does not say anything; just stares at us musingly, as if his mind were elsewhere. Salif tells him why we are here: to pay our respects, to have a chat. Still the Mayor seems distracted, stroking his chin.

'Hmm, yes, very good, very good,' he says. Then suddenly

he comes to himself. Perhaps he was contemplating his last interview, no doubt some tricky matter... a favor perhaps... perhaps a deal of some sort. Or maybe he is wondering how to respond to the question he knows we are going to ask about some match-funding the Mayor's office was supposed to produce for the primary school.

'We've had a difficult year,' he says, shaking his head, 'very difficult. The poor rains... the birds. The farmers are desperate and there have been budget cuts in all government departments, meaning less money for helping them. A very difficult year.' We discuss such matters for a bit.

'The seminar was very good,' he says at length, the beginning of which he witnessed. 'Excellent. You are working with all members of the community. This is very good. It is good that you show that this is what you are doing. People must realize that this work is not only for Salif's family. You know how these people are. They can be very jealous, very suspicious.'

'Of course. Our work is for the community as a whole,' Salif replies.

Has Demba Mody had complaints, I wonder, or is he just making his own point? I decide it is time to bring up the matter of the match-funding. We are buying books for the school and building a room to put them in, and the deal was that the Mayor's office would pay half the costs. This it has so far failed to do. I ask Demba Mody when the money might be available.

'Ah, this is a problem,' he exclaims. 'This is not good. We need to help the schools. The headteacher has been in here a number of times asking for things. He has even given me a letter. Alas, what with the government budget cuts, the Mayor's office has not received the finance we expected. We are hoping to get more. But for the moment we simply do not have any funds.' And, according to Salif, they never will, as Demba Mody, despite his initial commitment to the project, is not one to put education high on his agenda. I look at the Mayor and know Salif is right. This is a man of diplomacy, and there will always be bigger fish than headteachers; or ourselves, for that matter.

It is stiflingly hot in the Mayor's office and I am happy when, shortly after, we leave it. Demba Mody comes with us out to the front of the building.

'We appreciate the work Salif and you do in our community,' he says looking me directly in the eye. 'This is the work of Allah, and it is taken note of.' He is a man, I believe, who means well.

The primary school, to where we go next, had 700 pupils when I first visited it a few years ago, and only nine members of staff and seven classrooms. The teaching materials consisted of only a handful of exercise books – which the higher-grade children shared – a few blackboards and 10 teaching manuals. The headteacher, Sidi Khan, a quiet, committed man, devoted his life to doing the best he could for his students. He presided over the few decrepit buildings of the school from his small office, and in the evenings did the rounds of the family compounds, making sure his charges were doing their homework, helping them and relaying the few exercise books. We financed the provision of extra books and the construction of a number of desks, as in most classrooms the children had to sit on the floor. Then things improved. A change in government brought in a boost to the education budget. Were these the first signs of better things to come, of a governmental renaissance? Perhaps. A second primary school was even constructed, although Sidi Khan was sent off to some distant posting and I have not seen him for a number of years. Now, however, I am happy to hear from Salif that he is back and has been put in charge of this new school.

We pull up at the door to the school compound and go in.

The place is new and tidy, with two low, freshly painted rows of classrooms facing each other across an expanse of sand. Sidi Khan sees us from a classroom where he is teaching and comes out to greet us. Although polite and formal, he is warm and takes us over to his office where we talk of how the school is faring. They still lack resources and there are problems with the classroom floors, he says. The contractors who built the school, probably with the connivance of the managers who controlled the budget, so reduced the cement content of the concrete floors that they have already broken up and, if there is any wind, the rooms fill with dust.

'I took the Mayor a letter,' Sidi Khan says, 'stating this and listing all our other requirements. This was so it could not be denied that we have made our representations.' I do not know quite what he means by this but Sidi Khan is an intelligent man and I imagine that this is the next step in the game of chess that all who want something in Mauritania must play.

A little later, Sidi Khan leads us up the row of classrooms where, at our appearance in each doorway, 50 small faces stare at us in astonishment before their teacher orders them to stand. Two or three to a desk all jammed together on what is now a sand and dust floor, they immediately leap to their feet and chant out in unison: '*Bonjour, Monsieur le Directeur.*' The teachers look sweaty and overworked and Sidi Khan nods his head to each one as though he were a general inspecting his officers. The school is clearly strictly run under his authority. Teaching methods may definitely be of the 'old school' variety, the knuckle-wrapping ruler still very much in evidence and most learning done by rote, but, in his last year at the last school, Salif tells me, Sidi Khan managed an 80-per-cent leavers' pass rate, a remarkable feat in the circumstances.

Having decided we will devote the remaining school budget to fixing up the classroom floors and reblackening the already-faded blackboards, we take our leave of Sidi Khan. We have two further visits to make. The first of these is to a small shop in the marketplace. This is the workplace of Abou Tidane, a tailor, whom we find sitting at his sewing machine, pushing the foot pedal up and down as he feeds his material through. Abou Tidiane is a compact, cheerful man with the hands of a farmer and, at our appearance, his face creases into the biggest of smiles.

'Allah... welcome,' he exclaims getting immediately from his seat to shake our hands. He is an immensely likable and friendly man and I have come to give him a photograph I took of him and his family on my last trip. Although Abou Tidiane works in Keniéba, his home is a tent some five kilometers out of town, where he lives with his wife and their three disabled children. Having three severely disabled children is a massive disadvantage in somewhere as difficult as southern Mauritania, and how Abou Tidiane and his wife manage I have no idea. But the extent to which they love their three children is evidenced by his request that I photograph them and by the tender manner in which he lays his hands on their shoulders in the pose.

'Ah, truly, we look like Africans,' he laughs, when I give him the photograph.

Our final visit is to Salif's great uncle, an ancient of a hundred years according to Salif. Whether or not the old man has in fact achieved this milestone I do not know, and I doubt if anyone actually does, but he certainly has the look of one who harks from a different era. He is in a room at the back of a large, neat compound that is home to Salif's paternal aunt. The room is dark and empty except for the old man, who sits, like an idol, in the dim light on a mat on the earthen floor with his prayer beads. Once, he would have been a tall, strong man, but his long limbs and body are now rendered to little more than bone and sinew. He wears nothing but a loincloth wrapped about his middle, his head is bare and his brown leathery body glows softly in the golden light.

We enter the room and squat down. As Salif takes the old man's hand and goes through the formulaic greetings, the old man slowly looks up. His eyes are blue from cataracts and the paper-thin skin of his forehead is creased with strain. He mumbles the greetings, then rallies and reaches out to take my and Salif's hands. Now he mumbles a blessing, coughing periodically as he does so, a deep rattle in his thin chest. In a corner of the room, leant up against the wall is an ancient, flintlock musket, for the old man, Salif tells me, was once a hunter.

I think of the Africa he must have known: one connected to its long history; one little changed over millennia; one steeped in its own traditions and societal norms – hunters, *griots* or storytellers, crops in the fields, a passing *marabout*, migrations, early, easy deaths, ancient mud-built towns, the weekly market, rains, stories, endless herds; one that is now rapidly disappearing. It would have been a hard life, as there was little ease or physical comfort then, but it would have been one with certainties that now no longer exist. The old man lets go of our hands; pulls his own down his face in the motion of washing himself. We are blessed. We get up to leave. A woman enters.

'Old Father,' she calls to the old man. 'It is Salif and his Nasrani.' The old man nods his head.

'Salif... Oumar Boubou's grandson,' she says.

'Yes, yes,' the old man croaks.

'He does not remember much,' the woman says. 'But he is strong.'

I lie in my hut that night and think of the old man. I think of the peace and humility that was in his face and hope that when my time comes to end my journey on this earth, I too will have found such peace and humility.

11 Away

The journey north... How would Westerners cope?... The Saudi problem... Businesspeople in charge... Fish-market beach... Adrosso and Amadou again... Doorway to another world

Dawn: cockerels crowing; shrouded figures outside their rooms, sweeping the sand of yesterday's debris. Salif calls me early and we take a quick tea with Amadou Tall in the lounge. Mariam is up. She offers me her goodbyes.

'Give my blessings to all your family,' she says. 'When will your girls come to see us?' I think of all the cockroaches; the spiders. I'm not sure. 'Some day, I hope,' I say.

Amadou Tall shoulders my rucksack and carries it out back to where the Toyota is waiting. We are in. Mamadou is by the window and I shake his hand. Then we are off.

The return journey to Nouakchott is like a river draining into the sea: there is a gravitational pull and inevitability about it. We stop briefly in Kaédi, to refuel. As early as it is, already the town is busy, already the dust is up: the donkey-carts, the peasants with their produce, the merchants, the gunning vehicles, the beggars and madmen, all preparing for another day of toil. As dysfunctional and hard as life is here – with the powerful easily rising, as in any jungle, above the vulnerable, and poverty clawing at the very fabric of society

– I cannot help wondering just how we in the West would cope in similar circumstances. I fear we would not come out of it so well. I fear a breakdown of economy and reasonable authority would result in an orgy of self-preservation that would make this place look positively cozy.

We traverse the south; then turn north. It is roasting, and better to have the Toyota window at least partially closed, as the wind is so hot and desiccating. We pass the tented camps, the herders, the nomads with their prehistoric camels on the empty plains that are home to them. They pass and are gone. We make good progress despite the many roadblocks, which do not hold us up too much. At one of them an old man is disputing with a soldier.

'Your ID is out of date,' the soldier keeps repeating.

'So what?' the old man replies, 'so am I.'

Soon, the south, Keniéba, the farmers and their fields are in the past. Now we are in the surreal landscape of the dune seas. If we turned right, I think to myself, and drove a true bee-line to the northeast, we could go 2,000 or 3,000 kilometers before we came to another road: what a great chunk of untrammelled world. Of course, there would be people. As we ploughed our way across dune sea and plain, we would meet up with nomads and their herds on unexpected pastures only they knew were there, or traversing the empty wastes on journeys of necessity. We would stop and greet them and share a tea; then move on.

The hours elapse, and we are silent. I seem finally to have run out of questions for Salif. We stop for a break in the town of merchants on the road. They have not ceased their trading; they do not notice our passing. A child stands begging with an empty tin where we take our tea and eat some biscuits. As we leave, Salif gives the boy the remainder of the biscuit packet and immediately three others with tins descend on him, squabbling over the spoils. The tea shack owner shoos them off like pigeons. Their tins denote them

as the students of a Qur'anic school, required to beg for their meals: beggar scholars.

Amadou Tall seems unaffected by the drowsiness that nods my and Salif's heads. He sits up, eyes fixed on the mirage-shimmering distances into which the Toyota moves like an ant. Then finally the electricity pylons appear, looping off into the desert where they power the great pumps that suck up the fossil waters that service the capital from whence they have come. We are still an hour-and-a-half outside Nouakchott, but soon the traffic is thickening; shacks and half-built buildings appear beside the road. Suddenly, I notice a change in the atmosphere. It is no longer dry. My skin is sticky. It is humid: the sea.

The city accumulates; then we are in a traffic jam. There is still desert around, but also buildings and a dual carriageway of green minibuses: fuming, stationary, people hanging off them. It's all very sudden. We negotiate our way to the center of town, then out again south to Amadou's district. It is 1.30pm. We have made excellent time. We install ourselves in Amadou's rooms where only Fama, his wife, is present, curled up asleep with her infant on the floor.

Amadou: large, shaven head; pockmarked face; sensitive eyes. He appears, as he has some hours off from work. He settles down on the carpeted floor of the lounge to make tea but is uncommunicative until I address him.

'We need to buy a pneumatic drill for our wells project,' I say to him. 'Do you know anything about the drill-to-compressor power ratio?' This is technical stuff, at which I am hopeless. How big a drill should we buy for work at the bottom of a well; and so how big does the compressor then need to be? This is what I need to ask. I have some paperwork that I brought with me describing various well-digging methods. I have it out in front of me. Amadou looks over from his tea making.

'How deep will you be drilling?'

'Up to 50 meters,' I say.

'Hmm,' he muses. The tea is hot in his pot. He lifts it off the burner and starts pouring it into the tea glasses, mixing it back and forth from glass to pot and pot to glass, concentrating.

'There are some details of compressors here,' I say. 'But I cannot make sense of the specifications.' He puts the teapot down and gets up to come over.

'This is no good,' he says, looking at the papers. 'These compressors are under-rated for your use.'

'Do you think we could buy a powerful enough second-hand compressor here?' I ask.

'Maybe.' He sits down again and resumes his mixing. 'I'll email you some specifications. Maybe you should look for one in England and send it over.' He busies himself with the glasses. Shortly, he looks up: 'And these Islamists,' he says. 'What about these Islamists?'

'What about them?' I say.

'Ah…' he chuckles; then: 'Bin Laden… he was the first of them. He was a clever man, but a fool as well. He hurt the Americans. The first to do so. People respected him for that, even if they did not like him. He was a fool, though, because he thought America was the problem.'

'What is the problem?' I ask. He is tasting the tea now, daintily holding the small glass, half filled with froth, between his fingers. He flips open the top of the teapot, pours the rest back in and returns the pot to the burner.

'The problem is the Saudis,' he says. 'They're the real capitalists. It is they who manipulate the price of oil, upon which the whole of the capitalist system rests. And as long as everyone expects their cars to be filled each day with fuel, they will have governments who will deal with such people, or anyone else for that matter. Bin Laden himself was a Saudi. He came from one of the richest Saudi families. Do you know the Saudis are even here in Mauritania, buying up land?'

'Are they?' More Land Grabs.

'And we will sell it. Always the African is ready to sell what is not his.'

'Should they not sell these lands?'

'Tens of thousands of hectares they want. Who does it belong to, this land? They're clever. Of course, it belongs to the businesspeople who are selling it. At least they are the ones with the title papers. That's how it is. That's how things work here.' He returns his attention to his teapot, lifting it off the burner with a piece of paper to protect his fingers from the hot handle. He says: 'There is a well-known Senegalese journalist who said: "The African thinks only of his stomach. When it is empty, he looks to fill it. When it is full, he sits back and does nothing."' He chuckles again, deep and rumbling. 'It's true, is it not?' I cannot tell whether the question is rhetorical or not.

'There are improvements,' I say. 'At least people know what good governance is now; at least they have heard of it.' I am thinking of that word, transparency, so prominent now in politic-speak.

Amadou's tea is ready. He pours a thin stream from a great height into the two glasses where they sit on their metal platter. The froth froths and he cuts the stream short with a twitch of his wrist. He reaches the platter over for me to take a glass; he shakes Salif by the shoulder where, tired after our trip, he is dozing on a divan and offers one to him. We drain our glasses in quick sups and toss them back, rolling them across the floor.

'You know, when I was in Russia,' he continues, 'the people used to say: "we are happy because we are not dead". That was when the winter froze everything and there were power cuts and everyone was cold. They'd say it after a few drinks, as the Russians like to drink. In Africa it is the same. We are happy, even as our governments rob us. You see the people: they are smiling, laughing, aren't they?' This time the question definitely is rhetorical.

'They say governments are getting better,' he continues. 'I too have heard this. Maybe somewhere it is true. But what difference does it make? The poor will always get poorer. It is always the same businesspeople in charge.'

'It takes a long time for real change to filter through,' I say. I want to say: there is a different, more modern Africa out there, now. There's a new generation that is dynamic and worldly wise. One by one, they will oust the old regimes; they will secure the change that is happening for the better. But do I believe this? What about all those natural resources for which foreign governments will increasingly compete, willing, on the insistence of their consumers, to make deals with the type of people who do not have the common interest in mind, the type with a vested interest in protecting the status quo? What about the ideological battles – the 'war on terror' – and the realities of climate change and the pressures these will bring to bear? But against this there is always the majority who are not greedy, or corrupt, or stupid – those like so many of the farmers I have met, the sheer weight of whose courage, inventiveness and resilience will surely, one hopes, like water, wear down even the hardest of adversaries.

Amadou shakes his head, musing: 'Perhaps,' he says, 'God willing.'

At this moment Fama appears with a cloth. She does not speak, and we watch as she spreads the cloth on the floor. Shortly she is back with a platter of fish and rice and we gather around to eat, big Amadou cradling his tiny infant in his lap, feeding tiny morsels of rice into its mouth like a bird feeding its chick.

4.00pm: we have some shopping to do. I also want to visit the fish-market beach, the color and salty confusion of which somehow seem always an appropriate conclusion to each trip. And we have not forgotten our rendezvous with Monsieur Adrosso.

Salif needs a new mobile phone, as his current one is old and does not work properly. We go to the corner in the center of town where the phones are bartered on the sidewalk. Nearby are a number of stationery shops. I persuade Salif to accept some files, a calculator and a briefcase. He says he does not need them, but I have seen the piles of papers in his room. Then we head north, past the hospital and out across what used to be the empty salt plain that separated the fish-market beach from the rest of town, an area no-one thought would be of any use as it was just too salty, inhospitable and liable to flooding. Now it is entirely built up: a whole district of whitewashed condominiums and mini-palaces all already starting to dissolve back into the salt plain from which they sprung – all, Salif tells me, under water during last year's floods. And all, he says, built with bank money, whatever that means.

The beach in Mauritania is around 600 kilometers long: an unchanging slope of sand stretching almost the entire length of the coast. It is unmarked, unused and undistinguished in any way. Then, as though making up for this, it becomes all of a sudden for two kilometers a dash of intense color. Here are 2,000 traditional fishing vessels pulled up high on its slope; an infinitely diminishing perspective of tall, pointed prows; flags fluttering in the breeze; crowds, wandering and congregating; nets, stacks of pots and wooden shacks: a whole small world of fisherfolk and fish-based commerce.

Out to sea, more of the long, brightly painted fishing boats ride the swell, some anchored, some preparing for a two-or three-day expedition out over the horizon, some readying themselves for the dash over the breakers to the shore. Here, the moment these last touch ground, a crowd descends on them like crabs, their catch stored in a large wooden box to be quickly distributed: in mounds on donkey-carts for the bigger merchants, or relayed in fish boxes to the ice-packing warehouse, or carried off in basins on women's heads for the city markets of tomorrow. Sitting on one end of the boats while the other unweighted end is swivelled around, a dozen oilskinned crewmembers gradually sidle the boats up the steep incline of the beach, eventually slotting them into their places with the other vessels, some of which are so huge you wonder how on earth they could ever be so maneuvered.

Salif and I wander. We remove our shoes and let the sea wash over our feet. This is such a contrast to the interior, to the somehow orderly, meticulous life of the farmer. It feels carefree: luxurious. We wander beyond the last of the fishing vessels, past the rusting wrecks of three large trawlers embedded in the sand. This sea, this coast, is one of the richest fishing grounds in the world, and unfortunately, the world has realized it and is plundering it accordingly. Japanese, Chinese, European, Korean: they are all here, dredging the fish, allegedly running down the local fishing boats when they get in the way, paying large 'licence' fees to government ministers who talk a lot about how they will use the money. Meanwhile fish stocks decline and what was once the primary source of protein for one of the poorest countries in the world is now a dwindling resource to which locals are only allowed restricted access. It is a familiar story, one that illustrates all too clearly the difficulty of co-ordinating poverty alleviation with a moral basis across all the different governing institutions of a rapacious global economy, even when there is the will to do so. It is another in the endless list of exploitation stories that litter Africa and the world – a story, however, that, for now at least, is not mine.

We used to walk up the beach all the way to the port, some ten kilometers off, but we no longer do this: those were earlier, perhaps more carefree days. Instead, we turn back, shortly coming to a boat that has just come in off the sea, which we watch. There is a crowd milling about it, and the catch is being distributed. But here it is the fisherfolk themselves who are doing the ferrying, and in the strangest of fashions. They are stuffing as many of the fish as they can down their baggy oilskin trousers, having first tied the bottoms with bits of string. They are stuffing them in frantically, crazily: large dogfish, dozens of smaller ones; then they dash up the beach to deposit them in some unseen destination before returning for more. Fish are everywhere, spilling out of their trousers, slipping and tumbling onto the sand where scrabbles of small boys dive for them. Salif is giggling uncontrollably at the sight.

'Look, see,' he says, as one of the young men trundles past, fish protruding from even his shirt. 'The owner of the boat has failed to pay the crew. Ah, truly, they are taking matters into their own hands.' Tears of pure, light-hearted joy are streaming down his face.

Later, we sit and watch the sun slide into the sea as the market packs up for the day; then we are off to Monsieur Adrosso's. I do not know what to expect at Monsieur Adrosso's, as I have never been to his house before. I am disappointed. The old man greets us at the door to his comfortable villa with genuine warmth and enthusiasm – 'Monsieur Peter, Salif, so good to see you. How was your trip? I have a very special dinner for you' – and the dinner is indeed delicious – langoustine deep-fried in batter taken at the glass dining table in his modern lounge. But the manner in which he treats the servant who waits for us, clicking his fingers at him irritably when he gets things wrong, barking at him in a manner so very alien to the culture in which I have been submerged for the last eleven days, not to mention the derogatory way in which his taciturn son talks of 'the Blacks', mean that both Salif and I are relieved when we return to the cozier, more egalitarian world of Amadou's rooms.

Here, a full evening is in swing: Amadou, as usual, presiding over the tea; Isa, Salif's pretty other daughter who is in minor disgrace having had a child out of wedlock – a child Salif inevitably dotes on; Mustapha, the military nurse who told the story of his time in Algeria; any number of cousins, students and other hangers-on. Few of them may have jobs; fewer still any money in their pockets. For most of them the long hours of each day might represent a struggle of Herculean proportions, but they have in each other and in their culture of gentleness, discipline and acceptance, a security that is solid; one that, it is true, might breed a certain complacency, but also one that all of us, including the modern Africa that is coming, might learn from.

1.00am: my alarm. I have a three o'clock flight. I wake Salif where he is asleep in the lounge.

'Leave Amadou Tall,' he says.

'Isn't he driving?' I ask.

'No, Amadou is.' The other Amadou, he means: our host. This is strange. He has work tomorrow.

'Why is Amadou taking us?' I ask.

'I don't know,' Salif replies. 'He said that he wanted to.' That's all.

Salif wakes Amadou. We clamber into his vehicle. We are silent: tired and half asleep. The city is empty. We rumble over uneven sand; then bump up onto the tarmac. The long, neon-lit avenues lead us towards the airport. We come to a roundabout. Here there are a couple of soldiers standing beside the road. They wave at us to stop: a checkpoint. Then Amadou does something odd, reckless – something I have not seen anyone do in Africa before. He aims the vehicle at the soldier most prominently in the road and drives straight at him. The man just has time to leap out of the way. I gasp. Salif exclaims loudly. But we are past.

Amadou's gaze is fixed on the road: fierce. No-one speaks. We arrive at the airport and pull into the parking lot, Amadou's ancient, wheezing vehicle coming to a standstill like an old man taking his last breath. Amadou climbs out and hands me my rucksack. His face is stony: defiant.

'Okay?' I ask.

'Of course,' he replies brusquely; then suddenly his face clears and the warm, kindly look I know him so well by comes back. 'Don't worry about those soldiers,' he smiles. 'They are nothing.'

'But they can be dangerous,' I say.

Amadou laughs.

'Not so dangerous,' he replies. 'Not so dangerous.'

I part from Salif by the airport terminal beside which a cordon of soldiers with batons stands, preventing anyone without a ticket from entering. We embrace. I will not see him for a year. Then I turn, show my ticket, and am swallowed up in the doorway to another world.